A Year in a Yorkshire Kitchen

by
Hilary Whitbread

Dalesman Books · 1987

The Dalesman Publishing Company Ltd
Clapham, Lancaster LA2 8EB

First published 1987

ISBN: 0 85206 914 6

*To my husband John with thanks for all of
his encouragement*

Line drawings in the text are by Valary Gustard and Victoria Wright.

Printed in England by Knight & Forster Ltd., Leeds

Introduction

All of the recipes in this book have been devised by myself and tested in my own kitchen. The ingredients are easily available and on the whole quite economical. The methods are straightforward and do not involve any special techniques or equipment. I hope that they will give as much pleasure to the reader as they have given to me.

Hilary Whitbread

The recipes are arranged according to the season. An index on pages 71 and 72 groups the recipes by type of dish.

General Hints

When separating eggs remember always to separate them into two bowls then pour the white into a third bowl. This means that if you are separating a lot of eggs several whites are not spoilt if one yolk breaks.

When whisking egg whites for meringue topping be careful not to over-whisk or you will break down the structure of the egg and the cooked meringue will go watery.

Do remember that when giving home-made confectionary as presents the wrapping is almost as important as the sweets. So take time to find suitable boxes or dishes, line them with paper doilies and carefully cover with clingfilm. Fine ribbon can be used to add the finishing touch to the wrapping or to make decorative rosettes.

Perfect Shortcrust Pastry

(1) Do not over-rub the pastry or the fat will go oily.
(2) Knead lightly after the liquid is added to achieve a smooth dough.
(3) Roll out on a lightly floured surface, do not turn the pastry over and do not flour the top of the pastry, only the rolling pin.

Remember

Do not mix Metric and Imperial weights in the recipes, use either one or the other.

tsp=teaspoon
tbsp=tablespoon

January 1st – New Year's Day

As soon as possible after the New Year arrives we should welcome the First Foot into our homes. Traditionally he must be a dark stranger carrying a piece of coal, a little bread and a coin as gifts. These symbolize the warmth, food and wealth which we hope will be ours in the coming year. Custom also has it that as he is a bearer of good fortune he ought to enter the house by the front door. At such a festive time it might be wise to have some cocktail savouries in the house – ready for any dark strangers who may drop in!

Cheese Dominoes

4 oz plain flour	100 g plain flour
Pinch of salt	Pinch of salt
1 oz margarine	25 g margarine
1 oz lard	25 g lard
2 oz grated cheese	50 g grated cheese

Sieve the flour and salt into a bowl, rub in the margarine and lard. Add enough cold water to mix to a firm dough. Knead gently for a few minutes to give a smooth pastry. Roll out thinly into a large rectangle. Cut the rectangle in half and on one half sprinkle the grated cheese. Lay the second half of the pastry on top of the cheese, press firmly and cut into domino shapes. Place these dominoes on a lightly greased baking tray.

Cook at 180°C, 350°F, Gas Mark 4 for 10-15 minutes until pale golden in colour. Cool on a wire rack.

Tuna Savouries

Bread Shells

16 slices of wholemeal bread	16 slices of wholemeal bread
2 oz margarine	50 g margarine

Filling

1 tin tuna (7 oz)	1 tin tuna (198 g)
2 tbsp sweetcorn	2 tbsp sweetcorn
2 tbsp salad cream	2 tbsp salad cream
Salt and pepper	Salt and pepper

Bread Shells

Cut the bread into circles using a large scone cutter. Melt the margarine in a pan and carefully brush both sides of the bread circles with it. Lightly press the circles into patty tins.

Cook at 180°C, 350°F, Gas Mark 4 for 25 minutes. Cool on a wire rack.

Filling

Drain the tin of tuna and flake the fish into a bowl. Stir in the sweetcorn and the salad cream and season lightly. Fill the cold, baked cases just before serving.

This recipe can be rather wasteful of bread but any leftover crusts can be used for breadcrumbs.

Chicken Liver Pâté

2 oz butter	50 g butter
1 onion peeled and finely chopped	1 onion peeled and finely chopped
8 oz chicken livers	225 g chicken livers
Salt and pepper	Salt and pepper
1 tsp French mustard	1 tsp French mustard
1 tbsp brandy	1 tbsp brandy

Melt 1 oz (25 g) of the butter in a heavy frying pan. Gently fry the onion until it is soft and translucent but not brown. Roughly chop the chicken livers and add them to the pan along with the salt and pepper and the mustard. Cook gently for 5-7 minutes. Leave to cool. Liquidize until the mixture is smooth. Add the brandy and pack into a small bowl. Melt the remaining 1 oz (25 g) of the butter and pour it over the pâté. Cover with clingfilm and chill overnight.

Serve spread thinly on savoury biscuits.

Kipper Pâté

1 pkt boil in the bag kippers (7 oz)	1 pkt boil in the bag kippers (198 g)
Salt and pepper	Salt and pepper
1 oz butter	25 g butter
1 small onion very finely chopped	1 small onion very finely chopped
1 tbsp lemon juice	1 tbsp lemon juice
2 tbsp double cream	2 tbsp double cream

Cook the fish according to the instructions on the packet. Remove any skin and bones and pound the fish in a bowl. Season lightly.

Melt the butter in a pan and gently cook the onions until they are soft and translucent but not brown. Stir the onions and butter into the fish. Add the lemon juice and the cream and mix well.

Pack the mixture into a small bowl. Cover with clingfilm and chill overnight.

Serve spread on savoury biscuits.

January 5th—Twelfth Night

Nowadays this is traditionally the time by which all Christmas decorations must be taken down. In the past it was a night of great revelry when a large fruit cake was served. Hidden in the cake were a dried bean and a dried pea. The man who found the bean in his portion was 'King' for the night and the woman who found the pea was 'Queen'. This custom was lost in the eighteenth century and the cake was replaced by the Christmas cake which today is served earlier in the festive season.

As this is the last day of Christmas it is perhaps an ideal opportunity for using up any leftover mincemeat.

Apple and Mincemeat Pie

Filling

8 oz cooking apples, peeled, cored and sliced	225 g cooking apples, peeled, cored and sliced
2 oz granulated sugar	50 g granulated sugar
6 tbsp mincemeat	6 tbsp mincemeat

Shortcrust Pastry

6 oz plain flour	150 g plain flour
A pinch of salt	A pinch of salt
1½ oz margarine	40 g margarine
1½ oz lard	35 g lard
Cold water to mix	Cold water to mix

Glaze

1 egg white	1 egg white
A little castor sugar	A little castor sugar

Filling

Cook the apples in a covered pan over a low heat until they are soft and mushy, do not add water. Stir in the sugar and the mincemeat and leave to cool.

Shortcrust Pastry

Sieve the flour and salt into a bowl, rub in the margarine and the lard. Add enough cold water to mix to a firm dough. Knead gently for a few minutes to give a smooth pastry. Roll out half of the dough and line a lightly greased 7" (18 cm) pie plate with it. Spread the cold filling over the pastry on the pie plate. Roll out the second half of the pastry and lay it on top of the pie plate, trim the pastry, dampen the edges and press them together to seal them. Cut 3 vents in the pie with a pair of kitchen scissors.

Bake at 190°C, 375°F, Gas Mark 5 for 20 minutes.

Glaze

Take the pie out of the oven, brush it with the egg white and sprinkle it with a little castor sugar. Return it to the oven for 10 minutes. Cool on a wire rack.

Mincemeat Meringue Tarts

Shortcrust Pastry

6 oz plain flour	150 g plain flour
A pinch of salt	A pinch of salt
1½ oz margarine	40 g margarine
1½ oz lard	35 g lard
Cold water to mix	Cold water to mix

Filling

4 tbsp mincemeat	4 tbsp mincemeat
2 egg whites	2 egg whites
2 oz castor sugar	50 g castor sugar

Shortcrust Pastry

Sieve the flour and salt into a bowl, rub in the margarine and the lard. Add enough cold water to mix to a firm dough. Knead gently for a few minutes to give a smooth pastry. Roll out on a floured surface and cut into circles with a large scone cutter. Lightly grease 24 patty tins and line them with pastry circles.

Filling

Put a little mincemeat into the base of each tart.

Whisk the egg whites until they are stiff, fold in the sugar and whisk again until the mixture peaks. Put teaspoonsful of the meringue onto the tarts taking care to take it right to the edges of the pastry.

Bake at 190°C, 375°F, Gas Mark 5 for 20 minutes. Cool on a wire rack.

Plough Monday

This is the first Monday after January 6th and it was the date when farm work officially began again after the Christmas celebrations. However, it seems to have been such a day of merrymaking that I doubt whether much work would have been done. The Goathland Plough Stots are a reminder of this festival and today men pull a plough around the village accompanied by a group of sword dancers. As a concession to modern times this takes place on the first Saturday after Plough Monday. In the Goathland Hotel, Goathland, North Yorkshire, old photographs of these festivities can be seen.

Don't forget that January is the time for Seville oranges in the shops—so if you want a really tangy marmalade now is the time to make it.

Soups are ideal for the cold days of winter when they can be either a warming snack or a filling meal in themselves if they are served with thick slices of wholemeal bread—real peasant fayre, which is both nourishing and economical.

Chestnut Soup

8 oz chestnuts	225 g chestnuts
¼ oz margarine	7 g margarine
1 onion peeled and chopped	1 onion peeled and chopped
4 oz potato peeled and diced	100 g potato peeled and diced
1 pt chicken stock	600 ml chicken stock
Salt and pepper	Salt and pepper
1 bouquet garni	1 bouquet garni

(Made up of 6 peppercorns, a bay leaf, some dried sage leaves and a little blade mace tied in a piece of muslin.)

¼ pt milk	150 ml milk

Cut a vent in the skins of the chestnuts and boil them in some water in a covered pan for 15-20 minutes. Remove the skins.

Melt the margarine in a large pan and gently fry the onion until it is soft and translucent but not brown. Add the potato and fry for 5 minutes stirring frequently. Stir in the stock and season lightly. Add the chestnuts and the bouquet garni.

Cover and simmer gently for 15-20 minutes. Remove the bouquet garni.

Sieve or liquidize the soup. Stir in the milk and reheat to serve.

Frankfurter Soup

1 oz margarine	25 g margarine
2 onions peeled and chopped	2 onions peeled and chopped
8 oz potato peeled and diced	225 g potato peeled and diced
1 pt beef stock	600 ml beef stock
1 bay leaf	1 bay leaf
Salt and pepper	Salt and pepper
1 tin kidney beans (15 oz) rinsed and drained	1 tin kidney beans (425 g) rinsed and drained
1 tin frankfurter (hot dog) sausages (10 oz) chopped into 1″ pieces	1 tin frankfurter (hot dog) sausages (285 g) chopped into 2.5 cm pieces

Melt the margarine in a large pan and gently fry the onion until it is soft and translucent but not brown. Add the potato and fry for 5 minutes stirring frequently. Add the stock and the bay leaf and season lightly. Cover and simmer gently for 20 minutes. Stir in the kidney beans and the sausages and reheat.

Courgette Soup

1 oz margarine	25 g margarine
1 onion peeled and chopped	1 onion peeled and chopped
4 oz potato peeled and diced	100 g potato peeled and diced
1 lb courgettes sliced into rings	450 g courgettes sliced into rings
1 pt chicken stock	600 ml chicken stock
1 tin tomatoes (8 oz)	1 tin tomatoes (227 g)
1 tsp soy sauce	1 tsp soy sauce
1 bouquet garni	1 bouquet garni

(Made up of 6 peppercorns, a bay leaf, some dried sage leaves and a little blade mace tied in a piece of muslin.)

Salt and pepper	Salt and pepper
¼ pt milk	150 ml milk

Melt the margarine in a pan and gently fry the onion until it is soft and translucent but not brown. Add the potato and the courgette rings and fry for 5 minutes, stirring frequently. Add the stock, the full contents of the tin of tomatoes, soy sauce and bouquet garni and season lightly. Cover and simmer gently for 30 minutes or until all of the vegetables are tender. Remove the bouquet garni.

Sieve or liquidize the soup. Stir in the milk and reheat to serve.

Economy Tomato Soup

Soup

½ oz margarine	15 g margarine
1 onion peeled and finely chopped	1 onion peeled and finely chopped
1 tin tomatoes (14 oz)	1 tin tomatoes (397 g)
1½ pts chicken stock	900 ml chicken stock
1 tbsp tomato purée	1 tbsp tomato purée
1 bay leaf	1 bay leaf
Pinches of salt, black pepper and sugar	Pinches of salt, black pepper and sugar

Thickening

1 oz margarine	25 g margarine
1 oz plain flour	25 g plain flour
½ pt milk	300 ml milk
Salt and pepper	Salt and pepper

Soup

Melt ½ oz (15 g) margarine in a large pan and gently fry the onions until they are soft and translucent but not brown. Add the full contents of the tin of tomatoes with the chicken stock, tomato purée and bay leaf and season with pinches of salt, black pepper and sugar. Cover and simmer gently for 15-20 minutes. Remove the bay leaf and either sieve or liquidize the soup.

Thickening

Melt 1 oz (25 g) margarine in another pan, stir in the flour and cook gently for 2-3 minutes. Remove the pan from the heat and gradually stir in the milk, taking care to keep the sauce smooth. Return the pan to the heat and bring slowly to the boil, stirring continuously. Season and allow to simmer for 1 minute. Pour the sauce into the tomato soup and reheat to serve.

Kitchen Garden Soup

1 oz margarine	25 g margarine
1 onion peeled and chopped	1 onion peeled and chopped
8 oz carrot peeled and diced	225 g carrot peeled and diced
8 oz potato peeled and diced	225 g potato peeled and diced
4 oz parsnip peeled and diced	100 g parsnip peeled and diced
4 oz turnip peeled and diced	100 g turnip peeled and diced
4 oz leek washed and shredded	100 g leek washed and shredded
2 oz mushrooms washed and sliced	50 g mushrooms washed and sliced
2½ pt beef stock	1½ litres beef stock
½ tsp Worcester sauce	½ tsp Worcester sauce
Salt and pepper	Salt and pepper
1 bouquet garni	1 bouquet garni

(Made up of 6 peppercorns, a bay leaf, some dried sage leaves and a little blade mace tied in a piece of muslin.)

1 tsp tomato purée	1 tsp tomato purée
2 oz long grain rice	50 g long grain rice

Melt the margarine in a large pan and gently fry the onion until it is soft and translucent but not brown. Add the carrot, potato, parsnip, turnip, leek and mushrooms and fry for 5 minutes, stirring frequently. Stir in the stock and the Worcester sauce and season lightly. Add the bouquet garni and tomato purée and bring to the boil.

Cover and simmer for 15 minutes. Add the rice and simmer for a further 10 minutes. Taste to make sure that the rice is cooked before serving.

Smoked Haddock and Bacon Soup

½ oz margarine	15 g margarine
1 onion peeled and chopped	1 onion peeled and chopped
8 oz potato peeled and diced	225 g potato peeled and diced
1 pt chicken stock	600 ml chicken stock
1 bay leaf	1 bay leaf
Salt and pepper	Salt and pepper
8 oz back bacon cut into 1" squares	225 g back bacon cut into 2.5 cm squares
8 oz smoked haddock (thawed if frozen fish is used)	225 g smoked haddock (thawed if frozen fish is used)
A little milk for poaching the fish	A little milk for poaching the fish
1 tin sweetcorn (7 oz) rinsed and drained	1 tin sweetcorn (227 g) rinsed and drained
½ pt milk	300 ml milk

Melt the margarine in a large pan and gently fry the onion until it is soft and translucent but not brown. Add the potato and fry for 5 minutes, stirring frequently. Stir in the chicken stock and bay leaf and season lightly. Add the bacon. Cover and simmer gently for 15 minutes.

Gently poach the fish in a little milk for 15-20 minutes until it is cooked. Skin the fish and remove any bones. Flake the fish onto a plate. Add the cooked fish and the sweetcorn to the soup. Cover and simmer for a further 10 minutes. Stir in the milk and reheat to serve. Be sparing with the salt as the fish and bacon both contain quite large amounts of it.

February 1st – Candlemass Eve

The Christmas celebrations of the Church go on until Candlemass and in the past it was Candlemass Eve that was the traditional time when all Christmas decorations in the house had to be taken down.

February 2nd – Candlemass Day

On this day people took candles to church to be blessed. These candles were often kept throughout the year as they were thought to have magical powers against the forces of evil.

February 14th – St. Valentine's Day

It was believed that birds found their mates on this day and it became a time for lovers to exchange gifts and cards. This tradition is still kept up and a lovely Valentine present is a carefully wrapped box of homemade sweets. Perhaps you would like to try some of the following selection.

Almond Kisses

8 oz plain dessert chocolate	225 g plain dessert chocolate
3 oz margarine	75 g margarine
3 oz sieved icing sugar	75 g sieved icing sugar
1 tbsp golden syrup	1 tbsp golden syrup
3 oz ground almonds	75 g ground almonds
1 tsp almond essence	1 tsp almond essence

Melt 5 oz (150 g) of the chocolate in the bowl over a pan of hot water. Using petit four cases two at a time for extra thickness put some chocolate into each case and swirl it around to coat the base and the sides. Leave to set.

Cream the margarine and the icing sugar together. Beat in the golden syrup, ground almonds and almond essence. Fill the chocolate cups with this mixture.

Melt the remaining 3 oz (75 g) of the chocolate in a bowl over a pan of hot water and cover the filled chocolate cases with it, taking care to seal the chocolate right to the edges.

This makes 25-30 sweets.

Butterscotch Creams

8 oz plain dessert chocolate	225 g plain dessert chocolate
1 oz cornflour	25 g cornflour
¼ pt milk	150 ml milk
3 oz demerara sugar	75 g demerara sugar
1 egg yolk	1 egg yolk
½ oz butter	15 g butter

Melt 5 oz (150 g) of the chocolate in a bowl over a pan of hot water. Using petit four cases two at a time for extra thickness put some of the chocolate into each case and swirl it around to coat the base and the sides. Leave to set. Blend the cornflour in a bowl with a little of the milk. Heat the remainder in a pan with the sugar. Stir until the sugar dissolves and pour over the cornflour in the bowl. Mix well and return to the pan. Heat gently and stir continuously until the mixture simmers. Leave to cool a little then beat the egg yolk and the butter. Leave to cool. Spoon into the chocolate cups. Melt the remaining 3 oz (75 g) of chocolate in a bowl over a pan of hot water and cover the filled chocolate cases with it, taking care to seal the chocolate right to the edges.

This makes 25-30 sweets.

Coconut Favourites

6 oz margarine	150 g margarine
6 oz sieved icing sugar	150 g sieved icing sugar
12 oz desiccated coconut	300 g desiccated coconut
8 oz dessert milk chocolate	225 g dessert milk chocolate
1 tbsp olive oil	1 tbsp olive oil

Cream the margarine and gradually beat in the sieved icing sugar. Stir in the coconut. Roll into balls about the size of a large cherry. Melt the chocolate in a bowl over a pan of hot water and stir in the olive oil. Roll the sweets in the chocolate with a fork and put them on greaseproof paper to harden.

Coffee Cream Bonbons

4 oz plain dessert chocolate	100 g plain dessert chocolate
¼ pt double cream	150 ml double cream
1 oz castor sugar	25 g castor sugar
2 pinches of instant coffee powder	2 pinches of instant coffee powder
2 tbsp Tia Maria	2 tbsp Tia Maria
1 finely crushed chocolate flake	1 finely crushed chocolate flake

Melt the chocolate in a bowl over a pan of hot water. Using the petit four cases two at a time for extra thickness put some chocolate into each case and swirl it around to coat the base and the sides. Leave to set. Whisk the cream, castor sugar, instant coffee powder and Tia Maria until it peaks. Spoon this mixture into the chocolate cases. Lightly press the crushed chocolate flake into the cream and serve within 24 hours.

This makes 25 sweets.

Collop Monday

This is the day before Shrove Tuesday and it used to be a day when many of the good things in the kitchen were used up before the rigours of the Lenten fast. A traditional food on this day, as the name suggests, were collops.

Beef Collops

1 lb minced beef	450 g minced beef
1 onion peeled and chopped	1 onion peeled and chopped
1 oz plain flour	25 g plain flour
¾ pt beef stock	450 ml beef stock
1 bouquet garni	1 bouquet garni

(Made up of 6 peppercorns, a bay leaf, some dried sage leaves and a little blade mace tied in a piece of muslin)

Salt and pepper	Salt and pepper

Quickly brown the mince in a large pan. Lift the meat out of the pan and drain it well. Fry the onion in the fat that has come out of the meat and cook until it becomes soft and translucent but not brown. Stir in the flour and cook for 2-3 minutes. Remove the pan from the heat and gradually add the stock, taking care to keep the sauce smooth. Return the pan to the heat and bring to the boil stirring continuously. Return the meat to the pan, add the bouquet garni and season lightly. Cover and simmer gently for 30 minutes.

Serve on slices of wholemeal toast.

Shrove Tuesday

This was an important public holiday in the past and it has many traditions attached to it, the most popular one being the eating of pancakes. These were the fayre of this day because they used up any remaining eggs and fat which could not be eaten during Lent. In Scarborough a pancake bell was rung at St. Thomas' Hospital to tell the local women to start making their pancakes. Today this bell hangs in the museum and it is rung on Pancake Day each year. Another custom that is observed in Scarborough is the Shrovetide Skipping when in the afternoon young and old of both sexes skip on the shore and along the promenade.

Beefy Pancakes

Pancakes

4 oz plain flour	100 g plain flour
½ tsp salt	½ tsp salt
2 eggs	2 eggs
½ pt milk	300 ml milk
A little lard for frying	A little lard for frying

Filling

¼ oz margarine	7 g margarine
1 onion peeled and chopped	1 onion peeled and chopped
1 green pepper seeded and chopped	1 green pepper seeded and chopped
8 oz sliced roast beef cut into thin strips	225 g sliced roast beef cut into thin strips
1 tin water chestnuts (8 oz) rinsed, drained and chopped	1 tin water chestnuts (227 g) rinsed, drained and chopped
Salt and pepper	Salt and pepper

Sauce

½ oz margarine	15 g margarine
½ oz plain flour	15 g plain flour
½ pt beef stock	300 ml beef stock
1 tsp soy sauce	1 tsp soy sauce

Pancakes

Sieve the flour and salt into a bowl. Make a well in the centre and drop the eggs into it. Beat to a smooth batter, gradually adding the milk. Leave to stand for at least 1 hour. Melt a little lard in a pan and make 8 pancakes. Cool on a wire rack.

Filling

Melt the margarine in a large pan and fry the onion and green pepper until they are soft. Add the mushrooms and fry until they turn colour. Stir in the beef and the water chestnuts, season lightly and leave to cool. Stuff the pancakes with this cold mixture. Place them in a large casserole dish.

Sauce

Melt the margarine in a pan, stir in the flour and cook for 2-3 minutes. Remove from the heat and gradually stir in the stock and soy sauce. Return to the heat and bring slowly to the boil stirring continuously. Pour over the pancakes. Cover and cook at 180°C, 350°F, Gas Mark 4 for 30 minutes.

Cheese and Bacon Pancakes

Pancakes

4 oz plain flour	100 g plain flour
½ tsp salt	½ tsp salt
2 eggs	2 eggs
½ pt milk	300 ml milk
½ tsp dijon mustard	½ tsp dijon mustard
A little lard for frying	A little lard for frying

Filling

½ oz margarine	15 g margarine
1 small onion peeled and finely chopped	1 small onion peeled and finely chopped
8 oz smoked back bacon cut into 1″ squares	225 g smoked back bacon cut into 2.5 cm squares
1 tin tomatoes (8 oz) drained	1 tin tomatoes (227 g) drained
Salt and pepper	Salt and pepper
2 tbsp sweetcorn	2 tbsp sweetcorn

Sauce

1 oz margarine	25 g margarine
1 oz plain flour	25 g plain flour
½ pt milk	300 ml milk
Salt and pepper	Salt and pepper
3 oz grated cheese	75 g grated cheese
1 slice of breadcrumbs	1 slice of breadcrumbs

Pancakes

Sieve the flour and salt into a bowl. Make a well in the centre and drop the eggs into it. Beat the eggs and flour to a smooth batter, gradually add the milk and mustard. Make sure that the mustard is well blended. Leave to stand for at least 1 hour. Melt a little lard in a pan and make 8 pancakes. Leave the pancakes on a wire rack to cool.

Filling

Melt the margarine in a pan and gently fry the onion until it is soft and translucent but not brown. Add the bacon and fry until it changes colour. Chop the drained tomatoes and stir them in. Season lightly and simmer gently, uncovered for 30 minutes. Add the sweetcorn and leave to cool. Fill the pancakes with this cold mixture. Roll them up and put them into a lightly greased casserole dish.

Sauce

Melt the margarine in a pan, stir in the flour and cook gently for 2-3 minutes. Remove the pan from the heat and carefully stir in the milk taking care to keep the sauce smooth. Return the pan to the heat and bring slowly to the boil stirring continuously. Boil for a minute, stir in 2 oz (50 g) of the cheese and season lightly. Pour the sauce over the pancakes. Scatter the remaining cheese, mixed with the fresh breadcrumbs, over the top and cook at 180°C, 350°F, Gas Mark 4 for 45 minutes.

Brown under a hot grill.

Cherry and Almond Pancakes

Pancakes

4 oz plain flour	100 g plain flour
½ tsp salt	½ tsp salt
2 eggs	2 eggs
½ pt milk	300 ml milk
A little lard for frying	A little lard for frying

Filling

1 lb cooking apples, peeled, cored and sliced	450 g cooking apples, peeled, cored and sliced
2 oz granulated sugar	50 g granulated sugar
1 tin black cherries (15 oz) drained and stoned	1 tin black cherries (426 g) drained and stoned
1 oz ground almonds	25 g ground almonds
A little castor sugar for sprinkling	A little castor sugar for sprinkling

Pancakes

Sieve the flour and salt together into a bowl. Make a well in the centre and drop the eggs into it. Beat the eggs and flour to a smooth batter, gradually adding the milk. Leave to stand for at least 1 hour. Melt a little lard in a pan and make 8 pancakes, keep them warm on a plate in a low oven 120°C, 250°F, Gas Mark ½.

Filling

Gently cook the apples in a covered pan with no water until they are pulpy. Stir in the sugar, black cherries and ground almonds. Fill the pancakes with the warm apple mixture. Roll them up and sprinkle them with castor sugar just before serving.

Pancake Lasagne

Pancakes

4 oz plain flour	100 g plain flour
½ tsp salt	½ tsp salt
2 eggs	2 eggs
½ pt milk	300 ml milk
A little lard for frying	A little lard for frying

Filling

¼ oz margarine	7 g margarine
1 small onion peeled and very finely chopped	1 small onion peeled and very finely chopped
1 tin kidney beans (15 oz) rinsed and drained	1 tin kidney beans (425 g) rinsed and drained
1 tin sweetcorn (7 oz) rinsed and drained	1 tin sweetcorn (198 g) rinsed and drained
1 tin red brown (borlotti) beans (14 oz) rinsed and drained	1 tin red brown (borlotti) beans (400 g) rinsed and drained
Salt and pepper	Salt and pepper

Sauce

2 oz margarine	50 g margarine
2 oz plain flour	50 g plain flour
1 pt milk	600 ml milk
4 oz grated cheese	100 g grated cheese
Salt and pepper	Salt and pepper

Pancakes

Sieve the flour and salt into a bowl. Make a well in the centre and drop the eggs into it. Beat the eggs and flour to a smooth batter, gradually adding the milk. Leave to stand for at least 1 hour. Melt a little lard in a pan and make 8 pancakes. Leave the pancakes on a wire rack to cool.

Filling

Melt the margarine in a pan and gently fry the onion until it is soft and translucent but not brown. Remove the pan from the heat and stir in the kidney beans, sweetcorn and the red brown (borlotti) beans. Season lightly. Leave to cool.

Sauce

Melt the margarine in a pan, stir in the flour and cook gently for 2-3 minutes. Remove the pan from the heat and gradually stir in the milk taking care to keep the sauce smooth. Return the pan to the heat and bring slowly to the boil stirring continuously. Season lightly and stir in 3 oz (75 g) of the cheese. Layer the pancakes, beans and sauce in a lightly greased casserole dish. Top with the sauce and scatter on the remaining 1 oz (25 g) of grated cheese. Cook at 180°C, 350°F, Gas Mark 4 for 45 minutes. Brown off under a hot grill.

Pancake Gateaux

Pancakes

4 oz plain flour	100 g plain flour
½ tsp salt	½ tsp salt
2 eggs	2 eggs
½ pt milk	300 ml milk
A little lard for frying	A little lard for frying

Filling

½ pt double cream	300 ml double cream
2 oz castor sugar	50 g castor sugar
4 tbsp whisky	4 tbsp whisky
1 tin mandarin oranges (11 oz) drained	1 tin mandarin oranges (312 g) drained

Pancakes

Sieve the flour and salt into a bowl. Make a well in the centre and drop the eggs into it. Beat the eggs and flour to a smooth batter, gradually adding the milk. Leave to stand for at least 1 hour. Melt a little lard in a pan and make 8 pancakes. Leave the pancakes on a wire rack to cool.

Filling

Whisk the cream, castor sugar and whisky together until the mixture gently peaks. Sandwich the pancakes together with the cream and most of the oranges. Reserve a little of the cream and some of the oranges for decorating the top of the cake.

Ash Wednesday

The fasting of Lent begins today so what better time for some frugal, vegetable recipes?

Courgette Starter

½ oz margarine	15 g margarine
2 onions peeled and chopped	2 onions peeled and chopped
12 oz courgettes thickly sliced	325 g courgettes thickly sliced
1 tin tomatoes (8 oz)	1 tin tomatoes (227 g)
Salt and pepper	Salt and pepper
1 oz grated cheese	25 g grated cheese
1 slice of wholemeal bread made into breadcrumbs	1 slice of wholemeal bread made into breadcrumbs

Melt the margarine in a pan and gently fry the onions until they are soft and translucent but not brown. Add the courgettes and fry for 5 minutes. Stir in the full contents of the tin of tomatoes and season lightly.

Cover and simmer gently for 25 minutes. Simmer quickly for 5 minutes uncovered.

Pour into a heat resistant dish. Sprinkle with the grated cheese and breadcrumbs and brown under a hot grill.

Serve at once with lightly toasted wholemeal bread.

Country Fry-Up

2 oz margarine	50 g margarine
8 oz leeks chopped	225 g leeks chopped
4 tomatoes skinned and chopped	4 tomatoes skinned and chopped
Salt and pepper	Salt and pepper
12 oz cooked potato mashed with 1 oz margarine and 1 tbsp milk	325 g cooked potato mashed with 25 g margarine and 1 tbsp milk
2 oz grated cheese	50 g grated cheese

Melt the margarine in a large pan and gently fry the leeks for 20 minutes. Stir in the tomatoes and cook for a further 5 minutes. Season lightly. Stir this mixture into the mashed potato and return it to the pan. Fry until it is nicely browned on both sides.

Sprinkle with the cheese and put under a hot grill until the cheese bubbles.

Serve piping hot.

Southern Supper

1 oz margarine	25 g margarine
1 onion peeled and chopped	1 onion peeled and chopped
1 oz plain flour	25 g plain flour
½ pt chicken stock	300 ml chicken stock
¼ pt milk	150 ml milk
Salt and pepper	Salt and pepper
1 bouquet garni	1 bouquet garni

(Made up of 6 peppercorns, a bay leaf, some dried sage leaves and a little blade mace tied in a piece of muslin.)

4 oz mushrooms washed and sliced	100 g mushrooms washed and sliced
1 carrot peeled and diced	1 carrot peeled and diced
1 tin kidney beans (15 oz) rinsed and drained	1 tin kidney beans (432 g) rinsed and drained
1 tin sweetcorn and peppers (7 oz) rinsed and drained	1 tin sweetcorn and peppers (198 g) rinsed and drained

Melt the margarine in a large pan and gently fry the onion until it is soft and translucent but not brown. Stir in the flour and cook for 2-3 minutes. Remove the pan from the heat and gradually stir in the stock and the milk taking care to keep the sauce smooth. Season lightly, add the bouquet garni. Return the pan to the heat and bring to the boil, stirring continuously. Add the prepared mushrooms and carrot. Cover and simmer gently for 20 minutes. Stir in the kidney beans and the sweetcorn and peppers. Cover and simmer for a further 10 minutes. Remove the bouquet garni.

Serve hot on a bed of pasta.

Vegetable Medley

1 oz margarine	25 g margarine
1 onion peeled and chopped	1 onion peeled and chopped
8 oz mushrooms washed and sliced	225 g mushrooms washed and sliced
1 tbsp plain flour	1 tbsp plain flour
½ pt beef stock	300 ml beef stock
1 tin baked beans (7.76 oz)	1 tin baked beans (220 g)
4 small tomatoes skinned and chopped	4 small tomatoes skinned and chopped
6 oz parsnip peeled and diced	150 g parsnip peeled and diced
1 tsp yeast extract	1 tsp yeast extract
Salt and pepper	Salt and pepper
8 oz peeled potato	225 g peeled potato
2 oz grated cheese	50 g grated cheese

Melt the margarine in a pan and gently fry the onion until it is soft and translucent but not brown. Fry the mushrooms until they turn colour, stir in the flour and cook for 2-3 minutes. Remove the pan from the heat and gradually add the stock taking care to keep the sauce smooth. Stir in the baked beans, tomatoes, parsnip and yeast extract and season to taste. Heat to simmering point then pour into a casserole dish. Slice the potatoes very thinly and arrange them on top of the vegetables. Cover and cook at 180°C, 350°F, Gas Mark 4 for 45 minutes. Remove the lid and return to the oven for a further 20 minutes. Take the casserole out of the oven and sprinkle it with the cheese. Put under a hot grill until the cheese bubbles.

Mothering Sunday

The origins of this day lie in the custom of local people making pilgrimages to their Mother Churches, or cathedrals, during Lent. Later it became a holiday for those in service who were allowed to visit their mothers at this time. The custom then lapsed but was revived during the Second World War by American servicemen stationed in Britain who had their own Mother's Day tradition. As it is a day for family tea parties why not try some of the following recipes which are ideal for turning any tea-time into an occasion? If you want to be traditional you could make the simnel cake, which always used to be eaten on Mothering Sunday, although now it is associated with Easter.

No-Bake Crispies

2 oz margarine	50 g margarine
8 oz Mars bars roughly chopped	225 g Mars bars roughly chopped
2 oz rice crispies	50 g rice crispies

Melt the margarine in a pan and add the Mars bars to it. Stir until the Mars bars melt and the mixture is smooth. Remove the pan from the heat and stir in the rice crispies. Pour into a lightly greased 7″ (18 cm) square cake tin and leave to cool. Cut into squares when cold. Store in an airtight tin.

Peanut Butter Cake

Cake

9 oz crushed digestive biscuits	250 g crushed digestive biscuits
2 oz margarine	50 g margarine
3 tbsp golden syrup	3 tbsp golden syrup
2 oz peanut butter	50 g peanut butter
4 oz plain cooking chocolate	100 g plain cooking chocolate
2 oz raisins	50 g raisins

Icing

1 oz plain cooking chocolate	25 g plain cooking chocolate
1 oz peanut butter	25 g peanut butter

Cake

Grease a 7″ (18 cm) flan dish. Put the crushed biscuits into a bowl. Melt the margarine in a pan, add the golden syrup, peanut butter, chocolate squares and raisins. Stir until the chocolate melts. Pour over the biscuit crumbs and stir well. Press the mixture into the flan dish and chill in the refrigerator.

Icing

When the cake is cool melt the chocolate in a bowl over a pan of hot water. Stir in the peanut butter then pour the icing over the cake and smooth with a knife.

Chocolate Fudge Cake

Chocolate Cake

6 oz margarine	150 g margarine
6 oz soft brown sugar	150 g soft brown sugar
3 eggs	3 eggs
5 oz S.R. flour	125 g S.R. flour
1 oz cocoa	25 g cocoa
A little milk to mix	A little milk to mix

Fudge Icing

2 oz margarine	50 g margarine
2 oz sieved icing sugar	50 g sieved icing sugar
2 oz soft brown sugar	50 g soft brown sugar
½ tsp vanilla essence	½ tsp vanilla essence
½ tsp instant coffee powder	½ tsp instant coffee powder
½ oz cocoa	15 g cocoa
2 tbsp golden syrup	2 tbsp golden syrup
A little milk to soften	A little milk to soften
6 miniature chocolate flakes	6 miniature chocolate flakes

Chocolate Cake

Lightly grease and line with greaseproof paper a 9" (23 cm) round cake tin. Cream the margarine and sugar together. Whisk the eggs and beat them into the creamed mixture. Sieve the flour and cocoa together and fold them in. If the mixture is too stiff add a little milk. Spoon into the cake tin leaving a slight hollow in the centre. Bake at 180°C, 350°F, Gas Mark 4 for 40-45 minutes. Cool on a wire rack.

Fudge Icing

Cream the margarine and icing sugar together. Beat in the soft brown sugar, vanilla essence, instant coffee powder, cocoa and golden syrup. Add a little milk to soften. Spread over the cake and decorate with the miniature chocolate flakes.

Ginger Creams

Biscuits

4 oz S.R. flour	100 g S.R. flour
4 oz wholemeal flour	100 g wholemeal flour
½ tsp baking powder	½ tsp baking powder
1 tsp ground ginger	1 tsp ground ginger
4 oz margarine	100 g margarine
4 oz soft brown sugar	100 g soft brown sugar
1 egg	1 egg
A little milk to mix	A little milk to mix

Butter Cream

2 oz margarine	50 g margarine
4 oz sieved icing sugar	100 g sieved icing sugar
1 tbsp dark syrup	1 tbsp dark syrup
1 tsp ground ginger	1 tsp ground ginger

Biscuits

Put the flours, baking powder and ground ginger into a bowl and mix well. Rub in the margarine and stir in the sugar. Lightly beat an egg and add it to the mixture. Mix to a stiff dough, if necessary add a little milk. Roll out thinly on a lightly floured board and cut into circles with a scone cutter. Place the biscuits on a lightly greased baking tray. Bake at 180°C, 350°F, Gas Mark 4 for 10-15 minutes. Leave on a wire rack to cool.

Butter Cream

Cream the margarine and icing sugar together. Beat in the dark syrup and the ground ginger. Use this cream to sandwich the biscuits together in pairs.

Simnel Cake

Almond Paste

12 oz ground almonds	300 g ground almonds
6 oz sieved icing sugar	150 g sieved icing sugar
6 oz castor sugar	150 g castor sugar
1 egg	1 egg
1 egg yolk	1 egg yolk
A few drops of almond essence	A few drops of almond essence

Simnel Cake

4 oz margarine	100 g margarine
4 oz soft brown sugar	100 g soft brown sugar
2 eggs	2 eggs
6 oz S.R. flour	150 g S.R. flour
1 tsp mixed spice	1 tsp mixed spice
2 oz glacé cherries	50 g glacé cherries
2 oz flaked almonds	50 g flaked almonds
4 oz sultanas	100 g sultanas
4 oz raisins	100 g raisins
1 oz mixed peel	25 g mixed peel
A little jam and a little beaten egg for finishing off the cake	A little jam and a little beaten egg for finishing off the cake

Almond Paste

Mix the almonds, icing sugar and castor sugar in a bowl. Lightly whisk the egg, egg yolk and almond essence together. Stir the egg mixture into the ground almonds and knead until smooth. Wrap ⅔rds of the paste in clingfilm and put it to one side. Roll out the remaining ⅓rd into a circle slightly smaller than the tin.

Simnel Cake

Grease and line a 7″ (18 cm) round cake tin with 3 layers of greaseproof paper. Cream the margarine and sugar together until they are soft and fluffy. Whisk the eggs and beat them into the creamed mixture a little at a time. Sieve the flour and mixed spice together and carefully fold them in. Add the glacé cherries, flaked almonds, sultanas, raisins and mixed peel and mix well. Place half of the cake mixture into the tin. Smooth off and lay the almond ring on top of it. Spoon the remaining cake mixture into the tin and leave a hollow in the centre.

Bake at 160°C, 325°F, Gas Mark 3 for 2½ hours. After 1½ hours cover the cake with some brown paper to prevent the top from burning. Cool the cake on a wire rack.

Roll out half the remaining almond paste and cut it into a circle the size of the cake. Brush the cake with a little melted jam and lay the almond ring on it. Make the rest of the paste into small balls. Press these into the almond paste around the edge of the cake. Brush the top of the cake with a little beaten egg. Pop the cake under a hot grill until the marzipan top is nicely browned.

The marzipan balls represent the apostles on an Easter simnel cake.

Wholemeal Rock Buns

4 oz S.R. flour	100g S.R. flour
4 oz wholemeal flour	100 g wholemeal flour
Pinch of salt	Pinch of salt
½ tsp baking powder	½ tsp baking powder
3 oz margarine	75 g margarine
3 oz dark muscovado sugar	75 g dark muscovado sugar
2 oz currants	50 g currants
2 oz raisins	50 g raisins.
1 egg	1 egg
Milk to mix	Milk to mix

Put the flours, salt and baking powder into a bowl. Rub in the margarine and stir in the sugar, currants and raisins. Lightly whisk the egg and stir it into the mixutre with a fork, add a little milk if necessary to make a stiff dough. Place the mixture in rough forkfuls onto lightly greased baking trays.

Bake at 200°C, 400°F, Gas Mark 6 for 15-20 minutes until golden brown. Cool on a wire rack.

Walnut and Cherry Upsidedown Cake

2 tbsp clear honey	2 tbsp clear honey
1 oz whole walnuts	25 g whole walnuts
2 oz whole glacé cherries	50 g whole glacé cherries
6 oz margarine	150 g margarine
6 oz castor sugar	150 g castor sugar
3 eggs	3 eggs
6 oz S.R. flour	150g S.R. flour
Milk to mix	Milk to mix
Whipped cream to serve	Whipped cream to serve

Put the honey into a well greased 9″ (23 cm) round cake tin and swirl it around the base to evenly coat it. Arrange the walnuts and cherries in a pattern in the base of the tin on top of the honey.

Cream the margarine and sugar together until they are soft and fluffy. Whisk the eggs and beat them into the creamed mixture a little at a time. Sieve the flour and carefully fold it in. The mixture should be of a soft dropping consistency, if it is too stiff add a little milk. Spoon the mixture on top fo the walnuts and cherries and leave a slight hollow in the centre of the cake.

Bake at 180°C, 350°F, Gas Mark 4 for 45-50 minutes. Leave in the tin for 10 minutes before turning out on a wire rack to cool.

Serve cold with whipped cream. This cake with its topping of walnuts and cherries set in honey is very attractive.

Tea-Time Special

4 oz margarine	100 g margarine
4 oz castor sugar	100 g castor sugar
2 eggs	2 eggs
5 oz S.R. flour	125 g S.R. flour
1 oz desiccated coconut	25 g desiccated coconut
2 egg whites	2 egg whites
3 oz castor sugar	75 g castor sugar
4 oz desiccated coconut	100 g desiccated coconut

Lightly grease and line with greaseproof paper a 7″ (18 cm) square cake tin. Cream the margarine and the sugar together until they are soft and fluffy. Whisk the eggs and beat them into the creamed mixture a little at a time. Sieve the flour and carefully fold it in together with the coconut. Spoon the mixture into the prepared cake tin and level it off.

Whisk the egg whites until they peak. Fold in the sugar and whisk again until the mixture is stiff. Fold in the coconut. Spoon this on top of the cake mixture and level it off, spreading it right to the eges of the tin.

Bake at 180°C, 350°F, Gas Mark 4 for 1 hour. Leave in the tin for 10 minutes then carefully take it out and cool on a wire rack.

March 21st – Kiplingcotes Derby

This race takes place every year near Beverley in Yorkshire. It has been run since 1519 and is the only race in the world where the winner may take home less in prize money than the runner-up.

Passion or Carling Sunday

The traditional fayre for this day was carlings which are a type of dried pea. These were left to soak in water overnight, lightly seasoned and cooked in butter. Sometimes they were served as a savoury with a little vinegar and sometimes they were sweetened with sugar. Young people often told their fortunes with carlings – a few would be left in a dish then everyone would take one out in turn and the person to pick the last carling would, according to custom, marry first.

Although the days are lengthening and spring is definitely in the air, there can still be cold, frosty nights when a hot casserole-type meal is the perfect way to warm everyone up.

Black and Beefy Stew

1 lb stewing steak trimmed and cut into 1″ cubes	450 g stewing steak trimmed and cut into 2.5 cm cubes
1 tbsp seasoned flour	1 tbsp seasoned flour
2 tbsp cooking oil	2 tbsp cooking oil
1 onion peeled and chopped	1 onion peeled and chopped
4 oz black pudding roughly chopped	100 g black pudding roughly chopped
1 large carrot peeled and diced	1 large carrot peeled and diced
1 large parsnip peeled and diced	1 large parsnip peeled and diced
¾ pt beef stock	450 ml beef stock
1 tbsp Worcester sauce	1 tbsp Worcester sauce
Salt and pepper	Salt and pepper

Toss the meat in the seasoned flour. Heat the oil in a large pan and quickly brown the meat. Drain the meat and put it into a casserole dish. Gently fry the onion in the oil until it is soft and translucent but not brown. Add the black pudding, carrot and parsnip and fry for 5 minutes. Stir in the stock and Worcester sauce and season lightly. Bring to the boil then transfer to the casserole dish.

Cover and cook at 180°C, 350°F, Gas Mark 4 for 2 hours.

Brandied Liver and Bacon

1 oz margarine	25 g margarine
1 onion peeled and finely chopped	1 onion peeled and finely chopped
1 lb lamb's liver trimmed and cut into 1" cubes	450 g lamb's liver trimmed and cut into 2.5 cm cubes
8 oz back bacon cut into 1" squares	225 g back bacon cut into 2.5 cm squares
Salt and pepper	Salt and pepper
2 tbsp brandy	2 tbsp brandy

Melt the margarine in a large pan and gently fry the onion until it is soft and translucent but not brown. Cover and cook gently for 5 minutes.

Add the liver to the onion and quickly brown it. Cook for 5 minutes. Add the bacon and cook for a further 5 minutes. Season lightly. Stir in the brandy.

Serve on its own with wholemeal bread.

Sausage Risotto

1 lb sausages	450 g sausages
1 oz margarine	25 g margarine
1 onion peeled and chopped	1 onion peeled and chopped
6 oz long grain rice	150 g long grain rice
1 pt beef stock	600 ml beef stock
1 tin garden peas (10 oz) rinsed and drained	1 tin garden peas (283 g) rinsed and drained
1 tin sweetcorn (10 oz) rinsed and drained	1 tin sweetcorn (284 g) rinsed and drained

Grill the sausages until they are nicely browned then cut them into 1" (2.5 cm) pieces. Melt the margarine in a large frying pan and gently fry the onion until it is soft. Add the rice and fry for a few minutes without browning it. Stir in the beef stock, season lightly and simmer uncovered for 15 minutes. Add the peas, sweetcorn and sausages to the rice and simmer for a further 5 minutes. If necessary add a little extra hot water.

Pork Fillet With Parsnip and Apple

1 oz margarine	25 g margarine
1 lb pork fillet cut into 4 slices	450 g pork fillet cut into 4 slices
1 onion peeled and chopped	1 onion peeled and chopped
1 oz plain flour	25 g plain flour
1 pt chicken stock	600 ml chicken stock
Salt and pepper	Salt and pepper
12 oz roughly chopped parsnip	325 g roughly chopped parsnip
4 oz finely chopped apple	100 g finely chopped apple

Melt the margarine in a pan and quickly brown the slices of pork fillet. Lift them out of the pan and put them into a casserole dish. Gently fry the onion until it is soft and translucent but not brown. Stir in the flour and cook for 2-3 minutes. Remove the pan from the heat and gradually stir in the stock, taking care to keep the sauce smooth. Return the pan to the heat and season lightly, bring to the boil stirring continuously. Add the parsnip and cooking apple to the sauce and pour over the meat. Cover and cook at 180°C, 350°F, Gas Mark 4 for 1 hour.

Chicken and Almond Casserole

1 oz margarine	25 g margarine
4 chicken breasts cuts into 1″ cubes	4 chicken breasts cut into 2.5 cm cubes
1 onion peeled and chopped	1 onion peeled and chopped
1 pt chicken stock	600 ml chicken stock
1 tbsp tomato purée	1 tbsp tomato purée
Salt and pepper	Salt and pepper
1 bouquet garni	1 bouquet garni

(Made up of 6 peppercorns, a bay leaf, some dried sage leaves and a little blade mace tied up in a piece of muslin.)

1 oz flaked almonds	25 g flaked almonds
1 oz sultanas	25 g sultanas
1 eating apple peeled, cored and chopped	1 eating apple peeled, cored and copped
2 tsp cornflour	2 tsp cornflour

Melt the margarine in a large pan. Add the chicken and quickly brown it. Drain the chicken well and put it to one side. Gently fry the onion until it is soft and translucent but not brown. Stir in the stock, tomato purée, salt and pepper and the bouquet garni. Return the chicken to the pan. Cover and simmer gently for 15 minutes. After 15 minutes add the almonds, sultanas and apple to the pan. Cover and simmer gently for a further 20 minutes.

Blend the cornflour in a cup with a little cold water. Add some of the hot stock to the mixture and return it to the pan. Bring to the boil stirring continuously. Remove the bouquet garni.

Serve on a bed of rice.

Mince Casserole

¾ pt milk	450 ml milk
1 bouquet garni	1 bouquet garni

(Made up of 6 peppercorns, a bay leaf, some dried sage leaves and a little blade mace tied in a piece of muslin.)

1 lb minced beef	450 g minced beef
1 onion peeled and chopped	1 onion peeled and chopped
1 oz plain flour	25 g plain flour
Salt and pepper	Salt and pepper
2 tomatoes skinned and chopped	2 tomatoes skinned and chopped
4 oz mushrooms washed and sliced	100 g mushrooms washed and sliced
4 oz carrots sliced into rings	100 g carrots sliced into rings

Put the milk into a pan, add the bouquet garni and bring it slowly to the boil. Remove the pan from the heat, cover and leave for 30 minutes. After 30 minutes remove the bouquet garni.

Quickly brown the mince in a pan. When the meat is browned put it into a casserole dish. Gently fry the onion, in the fat that has come out of the meat, until it is soft and translucent but not brown. Stir in the flour and cook for 2-3 minutes. Remove the pan from the heat and gradually add the milk, taking care to keep the sauce smooth. Return the pan to the heat and bring slowly to the boil stirring continuously. Season lightly and add the tomatoes, mushrooms and carrots. Pour over the meat and stir well. Cover and cook for 1¼ hours at 180°C, 350°F, Gas Mark 4.

April 1st – April Fool's Day

This is the day for playing practical jokes on friends and family but only in the morning. If a joke takes place after mid-day then the joker is the fool as the rhyme tells us,
"April Fool's Day's past and gone,
You're the Fool and I am none.
Four farthings make a penny,
You're the biggest Fool of any."

Palm or Fig Sunday

Figs were eaten in great quantities on this Sunday. Gifts of figs were given to children and there were even Fig Fairs. I have used dates in my recipes as they are easier to obtain than figs.

Date and Honey Scones

12 oz plain flour	325 g plain flour
½ level tsp salt	½ level tsp salt
2 tsp baking powder	2 tsp baking powder
2 oz margarine	50 g margarine
2 oz castor sugar	50 g castor sugar
4 oz chopped dates	100 g chopped dates
1 tbsp honey	1 tbsp honey
¼ pt milk	150 ml milk

Sieve the flour, salt and baking powder together and rub in the margarine. Stir in the sugar and the chopped dates. Add the honey and milk and mix to a soft dough. Knead lightly and roll out on a floured board. Cut into circles with a scone cutter and place them on greased baking trays, brush the tops with milk.

Bake at 220°C, 425°F, Gas Mark 7 for 10-15 minutes. Cool on a wire rack.

Date and Hazelnut Cake

Cake

4 oz margarine	100 g margarine
4 oz soft brown sugar	100 g soft brown sugar
2 eggs	2 eggs
4 oz S.R. flour	100 g S.R. flour
1 oz hazelnuts finely chopped	25 g hazelnuts finely chopped
1 oz date finely chopped	25 g date finely chopped
Milk to mix	Milk to mix

Filling

2 tbsp apricot jam	2 tbsp apricot jam

Cake

Cream the margarine and sugar together until they are soft and fluffy. Whisk the eggs and beat them into the creamed mixture a little at a time. Fold in the flour, hazelnuts and dates. The mixture should be of a soft dropping consistency, if it is too stiff add a little milk. Spoon into a 7″ (18 cm) round cake tin which has been lined with greaseproof paper. Leave a slight hollow in the centre.

Bake at 180°C, 350°F, Gas Mark 4 for 45-50 minutes. Cool on a wire rack.

Filling
Cut in half when cold and sandwich the two halves together with the jam.

Breakfast Bonanza

2 oz hazelnuts	50 g hazelnuts
4 oz sultanas	100 g sultanas
1 oz chopped date	25 g chopped date
2 oz raisins	50 g raisins
1 oz currants	25 g currants
1 oz wheatgerm	25 g wheatgerm
1 oz soft brown sugar	25 g soft brown sugar
4 oz desiccated coconut	100 g desiccated coconut
12 oz rolled oats	350 g rolled oats
2 oz flaked almonds	50 g flaked almonds

Skin the hazelnuts by putting them under a hot grill for a few minutes and then rubbing them in a clean tea towel. Put the skinned nuts into a bowl. Add the dried fruit to the hazelnuts and stir in the wheatgerm and the sugar.

Mix the coconut, rolled oats and flaked almonds in a grill pan and gently toast them until they are lightly browned. Stir the toasted ingredients into the nuts and dried fruit in the bowl. Leave to cool.

Serve with milk. Store in an airtight tin.

Date and Ginger Pudding

4 oz margarine	100 g margarine
4 oz castor sugar	100 g castor sugar
2 eggs	2 eggs
2 oz S.R. flour	50 g S.R. flour
2 oz wholemeal flour	50 g wholemeal flour
½ tsp baking powder	½ tsp baking powder
½ tsp ground ginger	½ tsp ground ginger
1 oz date chopped	25 g date chopped
½ oz crystallized ginger chopped	15 g crystallized ginger chopped
A little milk to mix	A little milk to mix

Lightly grease a 1½ pt (900 ml) basin. Cream the margarine and sugar together until they are soft and fluffy. Whisk the eggs and beat them into the creamed mixture a little at a time. Fold in the flours, baking powder, ground ginger, date and crystallized ginger. The mixture should be of a soft dropping consistency, if it is too stiff add a little milk. Spoon the mixture into the basin and make a small depression in the centre of it. Cover the basin with two layers of greased, greaseproof paper and a layer of foil and tie with string. Pleat the greaseproof paper to allow room for expansion. Steam the pudding for 1½ hours.

Serve hot with custard.

Maundy Thursday

The reigning monarch has always given alms to the poor at this time, a tradition which our own Queen follows. As well as this royal occassion many parishes also had their own Maundy services, after which the poor were given alms.

Good Friday

Traditionally hot cross buns were baked in the morning and eaten during the day. The buns were marked with a cross and often some of them were dried in a warm oven and kept throughout the year, as they were believed to have magical healing powers. In some areas it was also thought that if they were kept then they would protect the house from the dangers of fire. The cross on the buns symbolizes the cross of Christ for us today. However, similar buns marked with a cross are known to have been eaten at this time of the year by both the Greeks and the Romans, who were pagans. Many places follow their own traditions on this day. For example, in Midgeley, a Pace-Egg Play is performed which shows the eternal struggle between good and evil.

Easter Monday

In many areas pace-eggs are given and rolled on this day. These are hardboiled eggs which have had their shells coloured. Today they will most likely to coloured by harmless, synthetic dyes but in the past flower petals and leaves were used. For instance, if the eggs are boiled with gorseblossom they turn yellow. The egg is the symbol of new life and a popular colour for the pace-egg is red which represents the blood of Christ. The name pace-egg probably derives from the word Paschal and the custom of colouring eggs is an old one as there is a mention of such eggs in the household accounts of Edward 1.

With pace-eggs and their modern equivalent, chocolate eggs, featuring so prominently at this time of the year I could not resist giving a selection of egg recipes here. If you are looking for a starter why not try Stuffed Hardboiled Eggs?

Stuffed Hardboiled Eggs

4 hardboiled eggs shelled	4 hardboiled eggs shelled
4 tsp thousand island dressing	4 tsp thousand island dressing
Salt and pepper	Salt and pepper
A little extra thousand island dressing	A little extra thousand island dressing.

Cut the hardboiled eggs in half lengthwise and carefully scoop out the yolks. Sieve the yolks, mix them with the thousand island dressing and season lightly. Spoon the mixture back into the hollows in the egg halves.

Serve with a little extra dressing trickled over the eggs.

The following recipes are suitable for tasty snacks or light lunches.

Baked Ham and Eggs

4 oz smoked ham chopped into 1″ squares	100 g smoked ham chopped into 2.5 cm squares
4 eggs	4 eggs
Salt and pepper	Salt and pepper

Lightly grease 4 small ovenproof bowls. Arrange the chopped ham in them. Break an egg into each bowl and season lightly with salt and pepper.

Cook at 230°C, 450°F, Gas Mark 8 for 10-15 minutes or until set.

Curried Omelette

½ oz margarine	15 g margarine
1 small onion peeled and finely chopped	1 small onion peeled and finely chopped
1 tsp curry powder	1 tsp curry powder
4 eggs	4 eggs
Salt and pepper	Salt and pepper

Melt the margarine in a large frying pan, cook the onion over a low heat until it is soft and translucent but not brown. Stir in the curry powder and cook for 2-3 minutes.

Lightly whisk the eggs with the salt and pepper. Pour them onto the onion in the pan. Increase the heat and cook until the omelette sets. Put under a hot grill to brown the top.

Bacon and Tomato Scramble

A nut of margarine	A nut of margarine
8 oz back bacon cut into 1″ squares	225 g back bacon cut into 2.5 cm squares
4 eggs	4 eggs
4 tbsp milk	4 tbsp milk
Salt and pepper	Salt and pepper
2 tomatoes skinned and chopped	2 tomatoes skinned and chopped

Melt the margarine in a frying pan and gently fry the bacon until it turns colour. Lightly whisk the eggs and milk together and season them. Stir the beaten egg into the bacon and add the chopped tomato. Cook slowly, stirring continuously until the egg hardens.

Serve on slices of wholemeal toast.

Potato Nests

1 lb potatoes peeled	450 g potatoes peeled
8 oz onions peeled and finely chopped	225 g onions peeled and finely chopped
1 oz margarine	25 g margarine
1 tbsp milk	1 tbsp milk
Salt and pepper	Salt and pepper
4 eggs	4 eggs
4 oz grated cheese	100 g grated cheese

Boil the potatoes and the onion in salted water for 15-20 minutes. Drain and mash them in a bowl with the margarine, milk and a little salt and pepper. Lightly grease a casserole dish and put the potato and onion mixture into it. Scoop out 4 hollows, each large enough to hold a poached egg.

Bring some salted water to the boil. Break the eggs and slip them quickly into the water. This will bring the water off the boil – do not boil again after the eggs have been added. The eggs will take between 3 and 5 minutes to cook depending on how well done you like them. When cooked remove them from the pan and place them in the 'nests' in the potato and onion mixture. Sprinkle the grated cheese over the dish and cook under a hot grill until the cheese is browned.

Savoury Flan

Shortcrust Pastry

6 oz plain flour	150 g plain flour
Pinch of salt	Pinch of salt
1½ oz margarine	40 g margarine
1½ oz lard	35 g lard
Cold water to mix	Cold water to mix

Filling

½ oz margarine	15 g margarine
1 onion peeled and chopped	1 onion peeled and chopped
1 green pepper seeded and chopped	1 green pepper seeded and chopped
8 oz back bacon cut into 1" squares	225 g back bacon cut into 2.5 cm squares
3 eggs	3 eggs
¼ pt milk	150 ml milk
Salt and pepper	Salt and pepper

Shortcrust Pastry

Sieve the flour and salt into a bowl. Rub in the margarine and lard and add enough water to make a firm dough. Knead gently for a few minutes to make a smooth pastry. Roll our and line a 9" (23 cm) greased flan dish with the pastry.

Filling

Melt the margarine in a pan and gently fry the onion and green pepper until they are soft. Lift them out of the pan and scatter them over the base of the flan dish. Gently fry the bacon until it turns colour, then scatter it over the onion and the pepper. Whisk the eggs and milk together and season lightly. Pour into the flan dish.

Cook at 190°C, 375°F, Gas Mark 5 for 45-50 minutes or until the flan is set and golden brown.

Serve hot or cold.

For dessert I have chosen a soufflé.

Orchard Soufflé

12 oz dessert apples peeled, cored and sliced	325 g dessert apples peeled, cored and sliced
2 oz castor sugar	50 g castor sugar
1 oz ground almonds	25 g ground almonds
2 egg yolks	2 egg yolks
3 egg whites	3 egg whites

Gently cook the apple in a covered pan over a low heat until it is soft and pulpy. Do not add any water to the apple. Stir in the castor sugar and the ground almonds and leave to cool. When cool stir in the egg yolks. Whisk the egg whites until they peak then fold them into the apple mixture. Lightly grease a 1½ pt (900 ml) soufflé dish. Pour the mixture into this.

Bake at 190°C, 375°F, Gas Mark 5 for 40 minutes. Serve hot at once.

May 1st-May Day

In parts of northern England May 1st is like April 1st, a day for practical jokes, but instead of the victim being called an April Fool he is called a May Gosling.

May 29th – Oak Apple Day

This day commemorates the restoration of Charles II to the throne and on it we are reminded of the day when the young Charles hid in an oak tree while fleeing from Cromwell's soldiers after the Battle of Worcester in 1651.

As the days become warmer and evenings lengthen we no longer feel the need to always have a hot meal. So now is the time to start serving salads. These are such versatile dishes and so easy to prepare that they need not be limited to the summer months but are especially useful at Christmastime when they can be made in advance and are ready to serve whenever you and your guests are ready to eat. There are two main types of salad. The first is a meal in itself and can easily stand alone, while the second is an accompanying salad and requires a selection of cold, sliced meats to be served with it.

Main Salads
Beefy Salad

Salad

8 oz cold roast beef cut into 1″ squares	225 g cold roast beef cut into 2.5 cm squares
1 onion peeled and finely chopped	1 onion peeled and finely chopped
1 tin beansprouts (9.9 oz) rinsed and drained	1 tin beansprouts (250 g) rinsed and drained
Salt and pepper	Salt and pepper
4 oz cooked beetroot diced (Do not use pickled beetroot)	100 g cooked beetroot diced (Do not use pickled beetroot)

Dressing

2 tbsp olive oil	2 tbsp olive oil
1 tbsp wine vinegar	1 tbsp wine vinegar
1 tsp soy sauce	1 tsp soy sauce
Salt and pepper	Salt and pepper

Salad
Put the meat, onion and beansprouts into a bowl. Season lightly and stir well.

Dressing
Put the olive oil, wine vinegar, soy sauce, salt and pepper into a screw top jar and shake well. Stir the dressing into the salad. Just before serving add the beetroot.

Friday's Salad

1 lb smoked haddock (thawed if frozen fish is used)	450 g smoked haddock (thawed if frozen fish is used)
½ oz margarine	15 g margarine
1 small cauliflower cut into small florets	1 small cauliflower cut into small florets
1 onion peeled and very finely chopped	1 small onion peeled and very finely chopped
2 oz mushrooms washed and thinly sliced	50 g mushrooms washed and thinly sliced
Salt and pepper	Salt and pepper

Dressing

3 tbsp olive oil	3 tbsp olive oil
1 tbsp white wine	1 tbsp white wine
A few drops of tabasco sauce	A few drops of tabasco sauce
Salt and pepper	Salt and pepper

Salad

Dot the fish with the margarine and gently steam for 20 minutes on a covered plate over a pan of boiling water. When cooked remove any skin and bones and flake the fish into a bowl. Leave to cool. When cold add the prepared raw vegetables and mix well. Season lightly but be careful not to add too much salt as smoked haddock can sometimes be quite salty.

Dressing

Put the olive oil, white wine, tabasco sauce and salt and pepper into a screw top jar and shake well. Stir the dressing into the salad.

Quick Salmon Salad

Salad

4 oz long grain rice	100 g grain rice
1 tin salmon (8 oz)	1 tin salmon (220 g)
1 small onion very finely chopped	1 small onion very finely chopped
3″ piece of cucumber diced	7.5 cm piece of cucumber diced
1 tbsp fresh chopped chives	1 tbsp fresh chopped chives
Cucumber rings for garnishing	Cucumber rings for garnishing

Dressing

1 tbsp olive oil	1 tbsp olive oil
1 tsp wine vinegar	1 tsp wine vinegar
1 tsp lemon juice	1 tsp lemon juice
Salt and pepper	Salt and pepper

Salad

Cook the rice in boiling, salted water for 10 minutes. Drain the pan and then fill it with cold water and drain it again as this makes the grains of rice separate. Put the rice into a bowl. Drain the tin of salmon, remove any skin and bones and flake it into the rice, stir in the onion and cucumber.

Dressing

Put the olive oil, wine vinegar, lemon juice and salt and pepper into a screw top jar and shake well. Stir the dressing into the salad. Just before serving garnish with the chopped chives and the cucumber rings.

Tuna Salad

6 oz long grain rice	150 g long grain rice
1 onion peeled and finely chopped	1 onion peeled and finely chopped
1 green pepper seeded and finely chopped	1 green pepper seeded and finely chopped
4 oz mushrooms washed and sliced	100 g mushrooms washed and sliced
1 tin tuna (7 oz) drained and flaked	1 tin tuna (198 g) drained and flaked
Salt and pepper	Salt and pepper

Dressing

2 tbsp corn oil	2 tbsp corn oil
1 tbsp wine vinegar	1 tbsp wine vinegar
Salt and pepper	Salt and pepper

Salad

Cook the rice in boiling, salted water for 10 minutes. Drain the pan then fill it with cold water and drain it again as this makes the grains of rice separate. Put the rice into a bowl and leave to cool. When cold stir in the onion, green pepper, mushrooms and flaked tuna. Season lightly.

Dressing

Put the corn oil, wine vinegar and salt and pepper into a screw top jar and shake well. Stir into the salad.

Dijon Salad

Salad

4 oz pasta spirals	100 g pasta spirals
1 lb cooked chicken cut into bite sized pieces	450 g cooked chicken cut into bite sized pieces
1 tin green beans (15.2 oz) rinsed and drained	1 tin green beans (430 g) rinsed and drained
Salt and pepper	Salt and pepper
4 tomatoes cut into wedges	4 tomatoes cut into wedges

Dressing

2 tbsp olive oil	2 tbsp olive oil
1 tbsp wine vinegar	1 tbsp wine vinegar
1 tsp Dijon mustard	1 tsp Dijon mustard
Salt and pepper	Salt and pepper

Salad

Cook the pasta in boiling, salted water for 10 minutes. Drain the pan then fill it with cold water and drain it again as this prevents the pasta from sticking to itself. Put the pasta into a bowl. Add the chicken and green beans to the pasta. Mix well and season lightly.

Dressing

Put the olive oil, wine vinegar, mustard, salt and pepper into a screw top jar and shake well. Stir the dressing into the salad. Make sure that the mustard is well blended. Just before serving garnish with the tomato wedges.

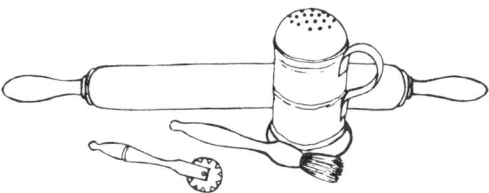

Supper Salad

8 oz mushrooms washed and sliced	225 g mushrooms washed and sliced
2 tbsp corn oil	2 tbsp corn oil
Salt and pepper	Salt and pepper
1 small onion peeled and chopped	1 small onion peeled and chopped
1 tsp lemon juice	1 tsp lemon juice
8 oz streaky bacon cut into 1″ squares	225 g streaky bacon cut into 2.5 cm squares
A little fat for frying	A little fat for frying
1 tbsp freshly chopped chives	1 tbsp freshly chopped chives

Gently cook the mushrooms in the corn oil for 10 minutes. Season them lightly and put the full contents of the pan into a bowl. Add the onion and lemon juice and mix well. Fry the bacon in a little fat until it is crisp. Drain well and pat dry on kitchen paper. Stir the bacon into the mushroom mixture. Sprinkle the salad with fresh chives and leave to cool.

Serve as a supper dish with wholemeal bread.

Accompanying Salads
Bean and Rice Salad

Salad

4 oz long grain rice	100 g long grain rice
1 tin red kidney beans (15 oz) rinsed and drained	1 tin red kidney beans (425 g) rinsed and drained
1 tin whole French beans (14½ oz) rinsed and drained	1 tin whole French beans (420 g) rinsed and drained
1 small onion peeled and very finely chopped	1 small onion peeled and very finely chopped
1 tbsp freshly chopped chives	1 tbsp freshly chopped chives
Salt and pepper	Salt and pepper

Dressing

2 tbsp olive oil	2 tbsp olive oil
1 tbsp wine vinegar	1 tbsp wine vinegar
Salt and pepper	Salt and pepper

Salad

Cook the rice in boiling, salted water for 10 minutes. Drain the pan then fill it with cold water and drain it again as this makes the grains of rice separate. Put the rice into a bowl and leave to cool.

Stir the kidney beans, French beans, onions and chives into the rice. Season lightly.

Dressing

Put the olive oil, wine vinegar, salt and pepper into a screw top jar and shake well. Stir the dressing into the salad.

Club Salad

¼ white cabbage finely
    shredded
1 oz raisins
1 oz finely chopped walnuts
1 tin pineapple (8¼ oz)
    drained and chopped
2 tbsp olive oil
1 tbsp lemon juice
3 tbsp salad cream
Salt and pepper

¼ white cabbage finely
    shredded
25 g raisins
25 g finely chopped walnuts
1 tin pineapple (234 g)
    drained and chopped
2 tbsp olive oil
1 tbsp lemon juice
3 tbsp salad cream
Salt and pepper

Put all of the ingredients into a bowl and mix well. What could be easier?

Fruity Side Salad

Salad

2 oz sultanas
1 tin pineapple chunks
    (8¼ oz)
6 oz long grain rice
Salt and pepper
3 oz dry roasted peanuts

50 g sultanas
1 tin pineapple chunks
    (234 g)
150 g long grain rice
Salt and pepper
75 g dry roasted peanuts

Dressing

2 tbsp olive oil
1 tbsp soy sauce
Salt and pepper

2 tbsp olive oil
1 tbsp soy sauce
Salt and pepper

Salad

Soak the sultanas for 2 hours in the juice from the tin of pineapple chunks. Cook the rice for 10 minutes in boiling, salted water. Drain the pan then fill it with cold water and drain it again as this makes the grains of rice separate. Put the rice into a bowl and leave to cool. Stir in the pineapple chunks, roughly chop them if they are too large. Drain the sultanas and add them to the salad. Season lightly and mix well.

Dressing

Put the olive oil, soy sauce, salt and pepper into a screw top jar and shake well. Stir the dressing into the salad.

    Toss in the dry roasted nuts just before serving so that they are crunchy.

Mushroom and Walnut Salad

8 oz mushrooms washed
    and sliced
⅛ pt red wine
Salt and pepper
1 oz walnuts roughly
    chopped
1 tbsp freshly chopped
    chives

225 g mushrooms washed
    and sliced
75 ml red wine
Salt and pepper
25 g walnuts roughly
    chopped
1 tbsp freshly chopped
    chives

Simmer the mushrooms gently in a covered pan with the wine and a little salt and pepper until they are tender. This should take approximately 10 minutes. Leave to cool.

    Put the mushrooms and the wine into a bowl, stir in the chopped walnuts and sprinkle with the chives.

Colourful Potato Salad

Salad

1 tin sweetcorn and mixed peppers (7 oz) rinsed and drained	1 tin sweetcorn and mixed peppers (198 g) rinsed and drained
8 oz cooked new potato diced	225 g cooked new potato diced
1 tbsp freshly chopped chives	1 tbsp freshly chopped chives
Salt and pepper	Salt and pepper
4 oz cooked beetroot diced	100 g cooked beetroot diced
(Do not use pickled beetroot)	(Do not use pickled beetroot)

Dressing

1 tbsp olive oil	1 tbsp olive oil
3 tbsp salad cream	3 tbsp salad cream
Salt and pepper	Salt and pepper

Salad

Put the sweetcorn and peppers into a bowl. Add the potato and the chives and season lightly. Mix well.

Dressing

Put the olive oil, salad cream, salt and pepper into a screw top jar and shake well. Stir the dressing into the salad. Just before serving stir in the beetroot.

Pineapple Salad with Curry Dressing

Salad

6 oz long grain rice	150 g long grain rice
1 tin crushed pineapple (8 oz) drained	1 tin crushed pineapple (227 g) drained

Dressing

½ oz margarine	15 g margarine
1 onion peeled and very finely chopped	1 onion peeled and very finely chopped
2 tsp curry powder	2 tsp curry powder
¼ pt salad cream	150 ml salad cream
¼ pt single cream	150 ml single cream
Salt and pepper	Salt and pepper

Salad

Cook the rice in boiling, salted water for 10 minutes. Drain well, fill the pan with cold water and drain again as this prevents the grains of rice from sticking to each other. Put the rice into a bowl and stir in the crushed pineapple. Put to one side.

Dressing

Melt the margarine in a pan and gently fry the onion until it is soft and translucent but not brown. Stir in the curry powder and cook for 2-3 minutes. Remove the pan from the heat and put the onion mixture into a bowl. Gradually stir in the salad cream and the single cream. Season to taste and serve with pineapple salad.

June 23rd – Midsummer's Eve

This was the night when bonfires burned all over the country to drive away evil spirits. Young people would leap through the flames for luck and it was believed that cattle would enjoy good health if they were driven through the dying embers of the fire.

With Midsummer upon us now is the time for picnics and picnic food. Salads such as those in the previous chapter can be packed into tupperware dishes and stored in a cool bag with a selection of cold meats.

Sandwiches and buns are always popular as they are easy to carry and here is a selection to add a little variety.

Cucumber and Cottage Cheese Buns

4 oz cottage cheese	100 g cottage cheese
Salt and pepper	Salt and pepper
4 large bread buns	4 large bread buns
Butter for spreading	Butter for spreading
¼ of a cucumber thinly sliced	¼ of a cucumber thinly sliced

Cream the cheese in a small bowl and season lightly. Cut the buns in half and butter them. Spread the bases of the buns with the cheese and top with slices of cucumber. Put the tops back on the buns.

Ploughman's Extras

6 wholemeal bread buns	6 wholemeal bread buns
Butter for spreading	Butter for spreading
4-6 oz cheddar cheese	100-150 g cheddar cheese
1 carton coleslaw (4 oz)	1 carton coleslaw (100 g)

Cut the buns in half and butter them. Slice the cheese and divide it between the buns. Divide the coleslaw and put it onto the cheese. Put the tops back on the buns.

Prawn Sandwiches

6 oz peeled prawns (thawed if frozen ones are used)	150 g peeled prawns (thawed if frozen ones are used)
Salt and pepper	Salt and pepper
1 tsp lemon juice	1 tsp lemon juice
1 oz softened butter	25 g softened butter

Beat the prawns, salt and pepper and the lemon juice to a paste in a bowl using a wooden spoon. In another bowl beat the butter until it is soft. Beat the prawns into the butter, an electric whisk at this stage will give a nice smooth texture.

Use as a sandwich filling. This amount will make approximately 4 rounds of sandwiches.

Delicatessen Ham Sandwiches

4 oz cooked ham thinly sliced into 4 slices	100 g cooked ham thinly sliced into 4 slices
A little butter for spreading	A little butter for spreading
8 slices of bread	8 slices of bread
A little sweetened stewed apple	A little sweetened stewed apple
A little finely sliced cucumber	A little finely sliced cucumber

Lay the ham on four lightly buttered slices of bread, spread with a little of the stewed apple and cover with a layer of cucumber. Top with the remaining four slices of lightly buttered bread.

Pastries are another standby for any picnic and although more care is required in carrying them they are tasty and can be served either on their own or with a selection of salad vegetables for a more substantial meal.

Sausage and Egg Pie

Shortcrust Pastry

6 oz plain flour	150 g plain flour
A pinch of salt	A pinch of salt
1½ oz margarine	40 g margarine
1½ oz lard	35 g lard
Cold water to mix	Cold water to mix

Filling

8 oz skinless sausages	225 g skinless sausages
3 eggs	3 eggs
Salt and pepper	Salt and pepper
1 tsp tomato purée	1 tsp tomatoe purée
A few drops of Worcester sauce	A few drops of Worcester sauce

Shortcrust Pastry

Sieve the flour and salt into a bowl, rub in the margarine and the lard. Add enough cold water to mix to a firm dough. Knead gently for a few minutes to give a smooth pastry. Roll out half of the dough and line a lightly greased 7" (18 cm) pie plate with it.

Filling

Grill the sausages until they are nicely browned. Chop them into 1" (2.5 cm) pieces and leave to cool.

Whisk the eggs, salt and pepper, tomato purée and Worcester sauce together.

Arrange the sausage pieces on the pastry-lined pie plate and cover with the egg mixture.

Roll out the second half of the pastry and lay it on top of the pie plate, trim the pastry, dampen the edges and press them together to seal them. Cut 3 vents in the pie with a pair of kitchen scissors.

Cook at 190°C, 375°F, Gas Mark 5 for 35-40 minutes.

Tuna and Cheese Pasties

Filling

8 oz potato peeled	225 g potato peeled
½ oz margarine	15 g margarine
Salt and pepper	Salt and pepper
1 tin tuna (7 oz)	1 tin tuna (198 g)
2 oz grated cheese	50 g grated cheese

Shortcrust Pastry

8 oz plain flour	200 g plain flour
Pinch of salt	Pinch of salt
2 oz margarine	50 g margarine
2 oz lard	50 g lard
Cold water to mix	Cold water to mix

Filling

Cook the potato in boiling, salted water for 15-20 minutes. Remove the potato from the pan, place it in a bowl and mash it with the margarine and a little salt and pepper. Drain the tin of tuna and flake the fish into the potato. Stir well. Leave to cool. When cool stir in the grated cheese.

Shortcrust Pastry

Sieve the flour and salt together in a bowl. Rub in the margarine and lard and add enough cold water to mix to a firm dough. Knead gently for a few minutes to give a smooth pastry. Roll out on a floured surface. Using a saucer as a pattern cut out 8 circles of pastry.

Divide the filling into 8 portions and place a portion on each of the circles. Smooth the filling into an oval shape. Dampen the edges of the pastry and pull up two sides of the circle into a pasty shape. Nip the edges together to seal them and crimp them between the thumb and forefinger. Prick each side of each pasty 3 times with a fork.

Cook at 200°C, 400°F, Gas Mark 6 for 25-30 minutes on lightly greased baking trays.

Most of us like to finish off a meal with something sweet. So do remember to pack some fruit or cake. The important point here is that whatever is taken on a picnic must be easy to carry and not too squashy. The cakes and biscuits that I have suggested are all fairly robust and there is no icing or buttercream that can become sticky or melt.

Honey Cake

5 oz margarine	125 g margarine
5 oz soft brown sugar	125 g soft brown sugar
3 eggs	3 eggs
2 tbsp clear honey	2 tbsp clear honey
8 oz S.R. flour	200 g S.R. flour
A little milk to mix	A little milk to mix

Grease and line with greaseproof paper and a deep 7" (18cm) round cake tin. Cream the margarine and sugar together until they are soft and fluffy. Whisk the eggs and add them to the mixture a little at a time. Beat in the honey. Sieve the flour and carefully fold it in. The mixture should be of a soft dropping consistency, if it is too stiff add a little milk. Spoon into the prepared tin and scoop out a depression in the centre.

Bake at 180°C, 350°F, Gas Mark 4 for 1 hour. Leave to cool in the tin for 5 minutes then turn out onto a wire rack.

Swiss Bars

2 oz margarine	50 g margarine
2 tbsp clear honey	2 tbsp clear honey
4 oz plain cooking chocolate	100 g plain cooking chocolate
8 oz muesli	200 g muesli

Melt the margarine in a pan over a low heat, add the honey and the choclate. Stir until the chocolate is dissolved. Remove the pan from the heat and stir in the muesli, taking care to ensure it is evenly coated. Press into a 7" (18cm) square cake tin which has first been lightly greased and lined with greaseproof paper. Leave to set. When set cut into bars.

Lemon Biscuits

8 oz S.R. flour	200 g S.R. flour
4 oz margarine	100 g margarine
4 oz granulated sugar	100 g granulated sugar
Finely grated rind of 1 lemon	Finely grated rind of 1 lemon
1 egg	1 egg
Milk for brushing	Milk for brushing
Castor sugar to dust	Castor sugar to dust

Sieve the flour into a bowl and rub in the margarine. Stir in the sugar and the finely grated lemon rind. Add the lightly beaten egg and mix to a stiff dough. Knead gently for a few minutes to give a smooth texture and roll out thinly on a floured board. Cut into circles with a scone cutter. Place on a lightly greased baking tray. Brush with milk and dust with castor sugar.

Bake at 180°C, 350°F, Gas Mark 4 for 15-20 minutes. Cool on a wire rack.

Uncle Sam's Brownies

3 oz margarine	75 g margarine
6 oz soft brown sugar	150 g soft brown sugar
2 eggs	2 eggs
½ tsp vanilla essence	½ tsp vanilla essence
3 oz S.R. flour	75 g S.R. flour
1½ oz cocoa	40 g cocoa
1 tbsp milk	1 tbsp milk
2 oz chopped walnuts	50 g chopped walnuts

Lightly grease a 7″ (18cm) square cake tin and line it with greaseproof paper.

Cream the margarine and sugar together until they are soft and fluffy. Whisk the eggs and beat them into the creamed mixture a little at a time along with the vanilla essence. Sieve the flour and cocoa together and carefully fold them in. Stir in the milk and the walnuts. Spoon the mixture into the cake tin and level off.

Bake at 190°C, 375°F, Gas Mark 5 for 30 minutes.

Leave the cake to cool in the tin for 5 minutes before turning it out onto a wire rack. Cut into squares when cold.

If you want to be very sophisticated you could take a dessert on your picnic. A fruit salad or a soaked fruit such as my recipe for Pineapple with Brandy and Orange Sauce is quite a good idea as it can be easily carried in a tupperware dish. I remember once taking some fruit and jelly on a picnic only to find that in the heat of the car the jelly had melted and had to be drunk rather than eaten! So beware and if you enjoy picnics and go on a lot of them it is certainly worth investing in a cool bag.

Pineapple with Brandy and Orange Sauce

1 tin pineapple chunks (14½ oz)	1 tin pineapple chunks (411 g)
Thinly cut rind of half an orange	Thinly cut rind of half an orange
½ pt water	300 ml water
2 tbsp golden syrup	2 tbsp golden syrup
4 tbsp pure orange juice	4 tbsp pure orange juice
2 tbsp brandy	2 tbsp brandy

Drain the pineapple chunks and place them in a bowl.

Put the orange rind into the water and leave it to stand for 20 minutes. Strain the water into a pan. Add the golden syrup and heat gently until it boils. Boil uncovered for 5 minutes then leave to cool. Stir in the orange juice and the brandy. Pour over the fruit and leave to stand overnight before serving.

July 4th – Old Midsummer's Eve

In 1752 the calendar was found to be inaccurate; the time was corrected but some days were lost. By the old calendar July 4th was Midsummer's Eve but by the new one it was June 23rd.

At Ripon, in Yorkshire, a curfew horn is blown every evening at 9 p.m. in the market place and outside what used to be the Mayor's house but is now a museum. This tradition dates back to the Anglo-Saxon period and in all of that time there have only been three curfew horns, the oldest dating from 886.

Midsummer sees an abundance of soft fruit both in the shops and in the garden and it is a time to preserve these fruits of summer so that they can be enjoyed in the dark days of winter. Today this is done either by freezing or jam making. My favourite home-made jam is raspberry which has a rich, deep, natural colour and a heavenly taste. It is also the time of the year when light, fruity desserts are in favour. So I have arranged an assortment of desserts suitable for the season.

Black Cherry and Chocolate Trifle

4 trifle sponges	4 trifle sponges
1 tin black cherries (15 oz) drained, stoned and halved	1 tin black cherries (425 g) drained, stoned and halved
1 blackcurrant jelly	1 blackcurrant jelly
1 oz cornflour	25 g cornflour
1 oz cocoa	25 g cocoa
¾ pt milk	450 ml milk
2 oz sugar	50 g sugar
1 egg	1 egg
¼ pt double cream	150 ml double cream
1 oz castor sugar	25 g castor sugar
1 tbsp white rum	1 tbsp white rum
A little grated chocolate	A little grated chocolate

Crumble the sponge cakes into a large bowl. Arrange the cherries over them. Make up the jelly, according to the instructions on the packet, and pour over the cherries. Leave to set. Put the cornflour and sieved cocoa into a basin and mix until smooth with a little of the milk. Heat the rest of the milk and when it is hot stir it into the cornflour mixture. Return this to the pan and gently bring to the boil stirring continouously to keep it smooth. Boil for a couple of minutes. Stir in 2 oz (50 g) of sugar. Remove from the heat and allow to cool a little. Beat the egg and mix it with a little of the cooled custard. Then stir it into the rest of the custard. Reheat, stirring all of the time, boil for a couple of minutes. Leave to cool a little then pour over the jelly. Leave to cool. Whisk the cream, castor sugar and white rum until it thickens. Spread over the custard and decorate with the grated chocolate.

Chocolate Banana Special

Chocolate Ice Cream

3 eggs	3 eggs
4 oz castor sugar	100 g castor sugar
1 pt milk	600 ml milk
4 oz plain dessert chocolate	100 g plain dessert chocolate
2 tsps vanilla essence	2 tsps vanilla essence
½ pt double cream	300 ml double cream

Chocolate Sauce

3 oz plain dessert chocolate	75 g plain dessert chocolate
A nut of butter	A nut of butter
A few drops of vanilla essence	A few drops of vanilla essence
½ pt water	300 ml water
3 oz castor sugar	75 g castor sugar
1 tbsp rum	1 tbsp rum
6 bananas	6 bananas

Chocolate Ice Cream

Lightly beat the eggs and sugar together. Warm the milk and pour this into the egg mixture. Return the sauce to the pan and heat gently stirring all of the time until the sauce thickens. It is not necessary to boil it but the sauce must be of a consistency that coats the back of the spoon. When it has thickened add the chocolate, broken into pieces, and the vanilla essence and beat until the chocolate has melted. Leave to cool. Whip the cream until it peaks and fold it into the cool sauce.

Put the mixture into a bowl and cover with clingfilm. Place the ice cream in the normal compartment of the refrigerator to set but before it sets stir it a couple of times to keep it smooth.

Chocolate sauce

Put the chocolate, butter, vanilla essence, water and sugar into a pan and heat gently until the chocolate melts. Boil quickly uncovered for 10 minutes. Allow to cool slightly then add the rum.

Slice the bananas in half lengthwise and serve them with scoopfuls of the ice cream and either hot or cold sauce. Do not peel the bananas until the dish is ready to be served or they will discolour.

Just before serving put the ice cream into the normal section of the refrigerator to soften a little.

Ice Cream and Butterscotch Sauce

Butterscotch Sauce

½ oz butter	15 g butter
1 oz soft brown sugar	25 g soft brown sugar
3 tbsp golden syrup	3 tbsp golden syrup
¼ pt double cream	150 ml double cream
A few drops of vanilla essence	A few drops of vanilla essence
A few drops of lemon juice	A few drops of lemon juice
1 family block of vanilla ice cream	1 family block of vanilla ice cream

Butterscotch Sauce

Gently melt the butter in a pan. Stir in the sugar and the golden syrup. Stir over a low heat until the mixture is smooth and the sugar has dissolved. Boil gently for 4 minutes. Remove the pan from the heat and stir in the double cream, vanilla essence and lemon juice. Stir until the sauce is quite smooth. Leave to cool. Pour over the ice cream just before serving.

Store the sauce in a screw top jar in the refrigerator.

Gooseberry and Ginger Crunch

Base

2 oz butter	50 g butter
2 oz soft brown sugar	50 g soft brown sugar
4½ oz crushed ginger nuts	115 g crushed ginger nuts

Gooseberry Cream

8 oz gooseberries washed, topped and tailed	225 g gooseberries washed, topped and tailed
2 oz castor sugar	50 g castor sugar
1 tbsp water	1 tbsp water
¼ pt double cream	150 ml double cream
2 egg whites	2 egg whites
2 oz castor sugar	50 g castor sugar

Topping

3 oz crushed ginger nuts	75 g crushed ginger nuts

Base

Melt the butter in a pan, stir in the sugar and the biscuit crumbs. Press the mixture firmly and evenly into the base of 4 individual fruit bowls.

Gooseberry Cream

Gently cook the gooseberries in a pan over a low heat with 2 oz (50 g) sugar and 1 tbsp water until they are soft. Drain off any excess liquid and leave to cool. Whisk the cream until it is floppy. In a separate bowl whisk the egg whites until they peak, fold in the sugar and whisk again until they are stiff. Fold the egg whites into the cream. Fold the cooked gooseberries into the cream and egg mixture. Spoon this onto the biscuit bases.

Topping

Just before serving sprinkle with the crushed biscuits.

Mocha Mousse

6 oz plain cooking chocolate	150 g plain cooking chocolate
1 tbsp strong black coffee	1 tbsp strong black coffee
1 tbsp Tia Maria	1 tbsp Tia Maria
4 eggs	4 eggs

Place a bowl over a pan of hot water, break the chocolate into squares and put them into the bowl to melt. Add the coffee to the chocolate and stir well. Remove the bowl from the pan and stir in the Tia Maria.

Separate the eggs. Beat the egg yolks into the chocolate. Whisk the egg whites until they are stiff then fold them into the chocolate mixture. Spoon into small dishes and leave in a cool place to set.

This mousse has a better flavour if it is not put in a refrigerator to set.

Normandy Syllabub

6 crushed meringue nests	6 crushed meringue nests
5 tsp cider	5 tsp cider
2 oz castor sugar	50 g castor sugar
Pinch of ground cinnamon	Pinch of ground cinnamon
½ pt double cream	300 ml double cream

Arrange the crushed meringues in the bases of 4 individual serving dishes. Put the cider, sugar and cinnamon into a bowl and stir well. Stir in the cream and whip until it is stiff. Spoon into the serving dishes and chill for 1 hour before serving.

This dessert does not keep well as the meringue goes soft if it is left too long.

Scrumpy Strawberry Trifle

4 trifle sponges	4 trifle sponges
1 lb fresh strawberries, hulled	450 g fresh strawberries, hulled
1 strawberry jelly	1 strawberry jelly
¼ pt cider	150 ml cider
1 oz cornflour	25 g cornflour
¾ pt milk	450 ml milk
2 oz sugar	50 g sugar
A few drops of yellow food colouring	A few drops of yellow food colouring
¼ pt double cream	150 ml double cream
1 oz castor sugar	25 g castor sugar
6 tbsp cider	6 tbsp cider
A few whole strawberries to decorate	A few whole strawberries to decorate

Crumble the sponge cakes into a large bowl. Arrange the strawberries over the sponge cakes. Make up the jelly according to the instructions on the packet but substituting ¼ pt (150 ml) of cold water with ¼ pt (150 ml) cider. Pour over the sponge cakes and the strawberries and leave to set.

Put the cornflour into a basin and mix until smooth with a little of the milk. Heat the remainder of the milk and when it is hot stir it into the cornflour mixture. Return this to the pan and bring gently to the boil stirring all the time to prevent it from going lumpy. Boil for a couple of minutes. Stir in the sugar and yellow food colouring. Remove from the heat and leave to cool a little. Pour over the jelly and leave to go cold.

Whisk the cream, castor sugar and cider together until the mixture is floppy. Spread over the custard and decorate with a few whole strawberries.

Strawberry Snow

8 oz strawberries washed and hulled	225 g strawberries washed and hulled
¼ pt double cream	150 ml double cream
2 oz castor sugar	50 g castor sugar
1 egg white	1 egg white

Mash the strawberries to a pulp. Whip the cream and sugar together until the mixture softly peaks. Whisk the egg white until it is stiff then fold it into the cream. Carefully fold in the strawberry purée and serve at once.

Strawberry Sunrise

1 lb strawberries washed and hulled	450 g strawberries washed and hulled
The strained juice of 2 oranges	The strained juice of 2 oranges
¼ pt double cream	150 ml double cream
1 oz castor sugar	25 g castor sugar
1 tbsp whisky	1 tbsp whisky

Arrange the strawberries in a large bowl. Pour the orange juice over them. Whip the cream, sugar and whisky together until the mixture gently peaks. Serve the cream with the strawberries.

If you have a sweet tooth a little sugar may be sprinkled over the fruit just before serving.

Midsummer Fancy

2 oranges	2 oranges
3 bananas	3 bananas
1 lb strawberries washed and hulled	450 g strawberries washed and hulled
¼ pt double cream	150 ml double cream
1 oz castor sugar	25 g castor sugar
1 tbsp white rum	1 tbsp white rum

Squeeze the juice out of the oranges and put it into a bowl. Peel the bananas and slice them into rings. Put the rings into the orange juice and toss them to make sure that they are evenly covered with the juice to prevent them from discolouring. Add the prepared strawberries and stir gently.

Whisk the cream, sugar and rum until the mixture gently peaks. Serve with the fruit. If you have a sweet tooth then a little sugar can be sprinkled on the fruit before serving.

Tipsy Fruit Salad

1 small melon	1 small melon
1 small pineapple	1 small pineapple
1 tin black cherries (15 oz) drained and stoned	1 tin black cherries (425 g) drained and stoned
4 tbsp brandy	4 tbsp brandy
½ pt double cream	300 ml double cream
2 oz castor sugar	50 g castor sugar
2 tbsp brandy	2 tbsp brandy

Halve the melon, remove the seeds, dice the fruit and put it into a serving bowl. Cut off the outer skin of the pineapple, slice the fruit into rings, remove the inner core, roughly chop the fruit and put it with the melon. Add the cherries. Pour the brandy over the fruit and leave to marinate for a couple of hours, stirring occasionally.

Whisk the cream, sugar and brandy together until the mixture peaks and serve with the fruit salad.

Raspberry Dream

2 oz plain dessert chocolate	50 g plain dessert chocolate
4 meringue nests	4 meringue nests
¼ pt double cream	150 ml double cream
1 oz castor sugar	25 g castor sugar
2 tbsp sherry	2 tbsp sherry
8 oz raspberries	225 g raspberries

Melt the chocolate in a bowl over a pan of hot water. Turn the meringue nests upsidedown and coat the outside of them thinly with the chocolate and leave to set.

Whisk the cream, castor sugar and sherry together until the mixture peaks.

Fill the meringue nests with all but 4 of the raspberries and top with the cream. Decorate each nest with one raspberry.

August 1st – Lammas

Lammas or Loaf Mass was a time when thanksgivings were said for the ripening grain. A number of loaves were made from the new wheat and blessed in Church.

I have taken this opportunity to give a few recipes which contain yeast so that in some way the traditions of Lammas as a bread-making time are kept alive. As well as this there are also ideas for tea loaves.

Yeast can now be obtained in three forms – fresh, dried and fast action. Fresh yeast must be creamed with some sugar, mixed with water and left until it is frothy. The dough has to rise/prove twice. Dried yeast is mixed with sugar and water and left until it is frothy. Once again the dough has to rise twice. Fast action yeast is added directly to the flour and only needs to rise once. Any kind of yeast can be used in any recipe as long as it is treated in the correct way. Although yeast recipes sound quite complicated the secret is not to rush the rising and the results are very rewarding.

Sausage Pizza

½ oz margarine	15 g margarine
1 onion peeled and finely chopped	1 onion peeled and finely chopped
1 tin tomatoes (8 oz)	1 tin tomatoes (227 g)
Salt and pepper	Salt and pepper
8 oz pork skinless sausages	225 g pork skinless sausages
2 oz grated cheese	50 g grated cheese
Generous pinch of oregano	Generous pinch of oregano

Dough

6 oz wholemeal flour	150 g wholemeal flour
2 oz plain flour	50 g plain flour
1 tsp salt	1 tsp salt
1 oz lard	25 g lard
½ oz fresh yeast	15 g fresh yeast
1 tsp sugar	1 tsp sugar
¼ pt tepid water	150 ml tepid water

Topping

Melt the margarine in a pan and gently fry the onion until it is soft and translucent but not brown. Drain the tin of tomatoes and add them to the pan. Season lightly and cook uncovered for 10 minutes. Leave to cool.

Dough

Put the flours and salt into a bowl and rub in the lard. Cream the yeast in a jug with the sugar and add the tepid water to it. Make a well in the centre of the flour and pour the yeast mixture into it. Leave in a warm place until the liquid is frothy. Stir the liquid into the flour with a wooden spoon. Knead well for 10 minutes. Put into a bowl and cover with a damp tea towel until it has doubled in size. Divide the dough in half and roll out two 7" (18 cm) circles. Put the circles onto lightly greased baking trays. Spread the cooled topping mixture onto the dough circles. Arrange the sausages on the pizzas and sprinkle with the cheese and oregano. Leave to prove for a further 15-20 minutes.

Cook at 200°C, 400°F, Gas Mark 6 for 25-30 minutes. Serve hot.

Italian Squares

Topping

½ oz margarine	15 g margarine
1 onion peeled and finely chopped	1 onion peeled and finely chopped
2 oz mushrooms washed and finely chopped	50 g mushrooms washed and finely chopped
1 tin tomatoes (8 oz)	1 tin tomatoes (227 g)
Salt and pepper	Salt and pepper
8 oz back bacon cut into 1″ squares	225 g back bacon cut into 2.5 cm squares
2 tbsp sweetcorn	2 tbsp sweetcorn
2 oz grated cheese	50 g grated cheese

Dough

6 oz wholemeal flour	150 g wholemeal flour
2 oz plain flour	50 g plain flour
1 tsp salt	1 tsp salt
1 oz lard	25 g lard
½ oz fresh yeast	15 g fresh yeast
1 tsp sugar	1 tsp sugar
¼ pt tepid water	150 ml tepid water

Topping

Melt the margarine in a pan and gently fry the onion until it is soft and translucent but not brown. Add the mushrooms and cook until they turn colour. Drain the tin of tomatoes and stir them into the onion and mushroom mixture. Season lightly and cook uncovered for 15 minutes. Add the bacon and sweetcorn and cook until the bacon turns colour. Leave to cool.

Dough

Put the flours and salt into a bowl and rub in the lard. Cream the yeast in a jug with the sugar and add the tepid water to it. Make a well in the centre of the flour and pour the yeast mixture into it. Leave in a warm place until the liquid is frothy. Stir the flour into the liquid with a wooden spoon. Knead well for ten minutes. Put into a bowl and cover with a damp tea towel until it has doubled in size. Roll out the dough to fit a lightly greased 10″ x 7″ (25.5 cm x 17.5 cm) tin. Spread the cooled topping mixture onto the dough, sprinkle on the cheese and leave to prove for a further 15-20 mins. Cook at 200°C, 400°F, Gas Mark 6 for 25-35 mins. When cooked cut into squares and serve hot or cold.

Cheese and Marmite Bread

8 oz wholemeal flour	225 g wholemeal flour
12 oz plain flour	325 g plain flour
2 tsp salt	2 tsp salt
4 oz grated cheese	100 g grated cheese
½ oz fast action yeast	15 g fast action yeast
½ pt warm water	300 ml warm water
A little marmite	A little marmite

Put the flours, salt, cheese and yeast into a bowl and stir well. Add the water and mix well with a wooden spoon. Knead for 10 minutes*. Roll into an oblong. Spread sparingly with a little marmite. Roll into a swiss roll shape and seal the joint well. Put onto a lightly greased baking tray, cover with a damp cloth and leave to double in size. Bake at 230°C, 450°F for 20-30 minutes. Cool on a wire rack.

*If fresh or dried yeast is used leave the dough in a bowl, covered with a damp tea towel, until it has doubled in size. Turn out and continue with the recipe.

Almond Ring

Filling

1 oz margarine	25 g margarine
1 oz castor sugar	25 g castor sugar
1 egg	1 egg
1 tsp cornflour	1 tsp cornflour
4 oz ground almonds	100 g ground almonds

Dough

1 tsp sugar	1 tsp sugar
¼ pt warmed milk	150 ml warmed milk
2 tsp dried yeast	2 tsp dried yeast
9 oz S.R. flour	250 g S.R. flour
Pinch of salt	Pinch of salt
1 oz margarine	25 g margarine
1 oz castor sugar	25 g castor sugar
1 egg	1 egg

Icing

2 oz sieved icing sugar	50 g sieved icing sugar
Warm water to mix	Warm water to mix
A few toasted, flaked almonds to decorate	A few toasted, flaked almonds to decorate

Filling

Cream the margarine and sugar together until they are light and fluffy. Whisk the egg and beat it into the mixture along with the cornflour and ground almonds.

Dough

Add 1 tsp sugar to the milk and stir gently until it dissolves. Add the dried yeast, stir well and leave in a warm place for about 10 minutes or until it is frothy. Sieve the flour and salt into a bowl, rub in the margarine and stir in the sugar. Pour the yeast liquid onto the flour, add the lightly beaten egg and mix to a soft dough. Knead the dough lightly on a floured surface until it is smooth. It is a very soft dough. Put it into a clean bowl, cover with clingfilm and leave in a warm place until it has doubled in size. When it has doubled knead it lightly.

Roll out into a rectangle approximately the size of a swiss roll tin and spread it with the filling leaving an empty border around the edges. Roll up along the long edge and seal well. Lightly grease a baking tray, join the two ends of the roll to form a circle and place it on the sheet. Cut the ring at 1″ (2.5 cm) intervals with a pair of kitchen scissors making sure that the cuts are deep, about ⅔rds of the way through the ring. Cover with a damp tea towel and leave to double in size. Bake at 200°C, 400°F, Gas Mark 6 for 30 minutes. The ring is very brown when it is cooked. Leave for 5 minutes on the baking tray before lifting onto a wire rack to cool.

Icing

Mix the icing sugar with enough warm water to give a coating consistency and ice the ring while it is still warm. Decorate with the toasted almond flakes.

This is best eaten on the day that it is made.

Sweet Chelsea Buns

Dough

1 tsp sugar	1 tsp sugar
¼ pt warmed milk	150 ml warmed milk
2 tsp dried yeast	2 tsp dried yeast
9 oz plain flour	250 g plain flour
Pinch of salt	Pinch of salt
1 oz butter	25 g butter
1 oz castor sugar	25 g castor sugar
1 egg	1 egg

Filling

1 oz butter	25 g butter

2 oz castor sugar	50 g castor sugar
2 oz raisins	50 g raisins
1 oz flaked almonds	25 g flaked almonds

Syrup

1 oz butter	25 g butter
2 oz soft brown sugar	50 g soft brown sugar
1 tbsp golden syrup	1 tbsp golden syrup

Dough

Add 1 tsp sugar to the milk and stir until it dissolves. Add the dried yeast, stir well and leave for about 10 minutes in a warm place, or until it is frothy. Sieve the flour and salt together. Rub in the butter and stir in the sugar. Pour the yeast liquid onto the flour, add the lightly beaten egg and mix to a soft dough. Knead the dough lightly on a floured surface until it is smooth. It is a very soft dough. Put it into a clean bowl, cover with clingfilm and leave in a warm place until it has doubled in size. When it has doubled knead lightly and roll out into a rectangle approximately the size of a swiss roll tin.

Filling

Spread the softened butter onto the rectangle leaving an empty border around the edges. Sprinkle on the sugar, raisins and flaked almonds. Roll up along the long edge, seal well and cut into 9 rings. Place the rings in a lightly greased 9″ (23 cm) round cake tin with the cut sides uppermost. Cover the tin with clingfilm and leave to rise until the rings have doubled in size.

Bake at 200°C, 400°F, Gas Mark 6 for 30 minutes. Leave the buns in the tin to cool for 10 minutes then turn them out onto a wire rack to cool.

Syrup

Melt the butter, sugar and golden syrup in a pan. Brush the syrup into the buns while they are still warm so that it soaks in.

These Sweet Chelsea Buns are best eaten on the day that they are made.

Tea-Time Loaf

Tea Loaf

4 oz raisins	100 g raisins
Juice of 1 orange	Juice of 1 orange
6 oz S.R. flour	150 g S.R. flour
3 oz wholemeal flour	75 g wholemeal flour
½ tsp bicarbonate of soda	½ tsp bicarbonate of soda
2 oz margarine	50 g margarine
3 oz soft brown sugar	75 g soft brown sugar
Finely grated rind of 1 orange	Finely grated rind of 1 orange
1 egg	1 egg
¼ pt milk	150 ml milk

Icing

4 oz sieved icing sugar	100 g sieved icing sugar
Enough fresh orange juice to mix to a glacé icing	Enough fresh orange juice to mix to a glacé icing

Tea Loaf

Steep the raisins overnight in the juice of 1 orange and the finely-grated orange rind. Line a 1 lb (450 g) loaf tin with greaseproof paper. Mix the flours and the bicarbonate of soda together. Rub in the margarine. Stir in the sugar and the soaked raisins, along with any remaining orange juice, and the orange rind. Beat the egg with the milk and add it to the mixture mixing well. The mixture is a very sloppy one. Put into the loaf tin. Bake at 160°C, 325°F, Gas Mark 3 for 1 hour. Cool on a wire rack.

Icing

Mix the icing sugar with enough orange juice to make a glacé icing. Glaze the tea loaf with this.

Banana Tea Loaf

Tea Loaf

4 oz plain flour	100 g plain flour
3 oz wholemeal flour	75 g wholemeal flour
1½ tsp baking powder	1½ tsp baking powder
½ tsp bicarbonate of soda	½ tsp bicarbonate of soda
Pinch of salt	Pinch of salt
1 oz lard	25 g lard
1 oz margarine	25 g margarine
4 oz soft brown sugar	100 g soft brown sugar
2 oz chopped almonds	50 g chopped almonds
3 bananas	3 bananas
A little milk to mix	A little milk to mix

Icing

4 oz icing sugar	100 g icing sugar
A little warm water to mix	A little warm water to mix

Tea Loaf

Line a 1 lb (450 g) loaf tin with greaseproof paper.

Mix the flours, baking powder, bicarbonate of soda and salt in a large bowl. Rub in the lard and the margarine. Stir in the sugar and the almonds. Mash the bananas in a separate bowl. Stir them into the mixture to give a soft, dropping, consistency. If the mixture is too stiff add a little milk.

Put the mixture into the loaf tin and bake at 200°C, 400°F, Gas Mark 6 for 30 minutes. Reduce the heat to 155°C, 310°F, Gas Mark 2 and bake for a further 45 minutes. Cool on a wire rack.

Icing

Mix the sieved icing sugar with enough warm water to make a glacé icing. Glaze the tea loaf with this.

Serve in slices with butter.

August 5th – Clipping the Church at Guiseley, Yorkshire

This ceremony takes place today because it is the day of the Church's patron saint, St. Oswald. The term 'clipping' means embracing and the church is embraced by the local people who join hands in a huge circle and slowly move around the outside of the building.

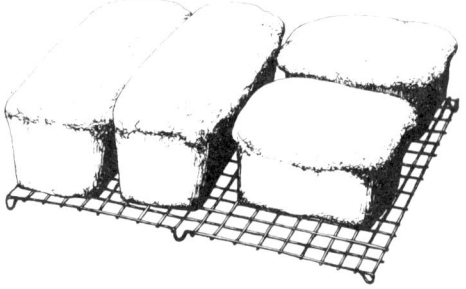

September 29th – Michaelmas

In the past men and women were hired by farmers at hiring fairs and were expected to work for a year. If after a year they wished to move on then this was the day that they did so. It was also supposed to be the day when the Devil spat on blackberries. So, if you are superstitious do not pick this fruit after today. Although, I personally find that bramble picking can be quite profitable until well into October.

Once again the evenings are beginning to draw in and there is often an autumn nip in the air. The light summer dishes are fading into memories and more hearty meals are called for. Traditionally England is famous for its pies and they are certainly ideally suited to autumn days. What could be more appetizing than a light, golden pastry covering a rich meat sauce; or if you have a sweet tooth you must try some of the sweet pies for dessert. Forget about the diet – prepare for winter!

Savoury Pies

Individual Shepherd's Pies

1 lb minced beef	450 g minced beef
1 onion peeled and chopped	1 onion peeled and chopped
1 tin tomatoes (8 oz)	1 tin tomatoes (227 g)
1 tsp Worcester sauce	1 tsp Worcester sauce
Generous pinch of mixed herbs	Generous pinch of mixed herbs
¼ pt beef stock	150 ml beef stock
Salt and pepper	Salt and pepper
1 tin sweetcorn (7 oz) rinsed and drained	1 tin sweetcorn (198 g) rinsed and drained
1 tsp cornflour	1 tsp cornflour
1 lb cooked potato mashed with 1 oz margarine, 1 tbsp milk and a little salt and pepper	450 g cooked potato mashed with 25 g margarine, 1 tbsp milk and a little salt and pepper
A little beaten egg for glazing	A little beaten egg for glazing

Brown the mince in a large pan. Add the onion and cook gently until it becomes soft and translucent but not brown. Stir in the full contents of the tin of tomatoes, roughly chopped. Add the Worcester sauce, mixed herbs and beef stock and season lightly. Cover and simmer gently for 30 minutes. Add the sweetcorn and reheat. Blend the cornflour with a little cold water in a cup. Stir in some of the hot stock and return it to the pan. Bring to the boil, stirring continuously. Pour into 4-6 individual ovenproof dishes. Top the meat with the mashed potato and brush with a little beaten egg.

Brown off under a hot grill.

Cheesy Meat Pie

Filling

12 oz minced beef	350 g minced beef
4 rashers of bacon cut into 1″ pieces	4 rashers of bacon cut into 2.5 cm pieces
1 onion peeled and chopped	1 onion peeled and chopped
4 oz mushrooms washed and sliced	100 g mushrooms washed and sliced
1 tbsp plain flour	1 tbsp plain flour
¾ pt beef stock	450 ml beef stock
Salt and pepper	Salt and pepper

Cheese Pastry

8 oz plain flour	200 g plain flour
Pinch of salt	Pinch of salt
2 oz margarine	50 g margarine
2 oz lard	50 g lard
2 oz grated cheese	50 g grated cheese
Cold water to mix	Cold water to mix
A little extra grated cheese	A little extra grated cheese

Filling

Brown the mince in a large pan then lift it out. Fry the bacon in the fat that has come out of the mince until it changes colour and put it with the mince. Gently fry the onion until it is soft and translucent but not brown, add the mushrooms and fry until they turn colour. Stir in the flour and cook for 2-3 minutes. Remove the pan from the heat and gradually stir in the stock taking care to keep the sauce smooth. Return the pan to the heat and bring to the boil stirring continuously. Return the mince and bacon to the pan and season to taste. Cover and simmer gently for 30 minutes. Leave to cool.

Cheese Pastry

Sieve the flour and salt into a bowl. Rub in the margarine and lard. Stir in the cheese and mix to a firm dough with cold water. Knead lightly to ensure a smooth pastry. Lightly grease a 9″ (23 cm) pie plate. Roll out half of the pastry and line the pie plate with it.

Spoon the cold meat sauce onto the pastry-lined pie plate. Roll out the remaining pastry and lay it on top of the plate. Trim it to fit, dampen the edges and seal them well. Cut 3 vents in the top of the pie with kitchen scissors. Sprinkle the pie with a little extra grated cheese.

Cook at 200°C, 400°F, Gas Mark 6 for 30 minutes.

Chicken Wellingtons

1 oz butter	25 g butter
4 chicken breasts skinned and boned	4 chicken breasts skinned and boned
1 onion peeled and very finely chopped	1 onion peeled and very finely chopped
2 tbsp whisky	2 tbsp whisky
4 oz mushrooms washed and finely chopped	100 g mushrooms washed and finely chopped
Salt and pepper	Salt and pepper
1 pkt frozen puff pastry (13 oz)	1 pkt frozen puff pastry (370 g)
A little beaten egg	A little beaten egg

Melt the butter in a frying pan and quickly brown the chicken breasts on both sides. Lift the meat out of the pan and leave it to cool. Gently fry the onion until it is soft and translucent but not brown. Add the whisky and mushrooms and fry until they turn colour. Season lightly. Lift the vegetables out of the pan, drain well and leave to cool. Roll out the pastry and cut into 4 squares. Place ¼ of the vegetable mixture on the centre of each square. Lay the chicken breasts on top of this. Fold the corners of the pastry up over the meat and bring to a point. Dampen the edges and nip them together to seal them, thus making a pastry parcel. Cut a couple of vents in the parcel and brush with a little beaten egg. Place on lightly greased baking trays.

Cook at 210°C, 425°F, Gas Mark 7 for 20 minutes.

Chicken Vol-au-Vents

1 oz butter	25 g butter
1 small onion finely chopped	1 small onion finely chopped
1 small green pepper seeded and finely chopped	1 small green pepper seeded and finely chopped
4 oz mushrooms finely chopped	100 g mushrooms finely chopped
4 tomatoes skinned and chopped	4 tomatoes skinned and chopped
Salt and pepper	Salt and pepper
8 oz cooked chicken, diced	225 g cooked chicken, diced
1 tsp oregano	1 tsp oregano
1 pkt of 12 frozen vol-au-vents	1 pkt of 12 frozen vol-au-vents

Melt the butter in a pan and fry the onion and green pepper until they are soft and translucent but not brown. Add the mushrooms and the tomatoes, season to taste, cover and simmer gently for 20 minutes. Stir in the chicken and oregano and cook for a further 10 minutes.

Bake the vol-au-vent cases as directed on the packet. Remove the tops, fill the cases with the chicken mixture and replace the tops.

Serve immediately as the filling softens the cases.

Mince Savoury Roll

8 oz minced beef	225 g minced beef
½ an onion finely chopped	½ an onion finely chopped
2 oz mushrooms finely chopped	50 g mushrooms finely chopped
½ tin tomatoes (8 oz)	½ tin tomatoes (227 g)
Salt and pepper	Salt and pepper
A few drops of tabasco sauce	A few drops of tabasco sauce
1½ oz wholemeal breadcrumbs	40 g wholemeal breadcrumbs
1 pkt frozen puff pastry (7½ oz)	1 pkt frozen puff pastry (213 g)
A little beaten egg to glaze	A little beaten egg to glaze

Brown the mince in a pan. Add the onion and fry gently until it becomes soft and translucent but not brown. Stir in the mushrooms and cook until they turn colour. Add the tomatoes. Season lightly and stir in the tabasco sauce. Simmer, uncovered, for 30 minutes. Leave to cool. Stir in the breadcrumbs.

Roll out the pastry into a large rectangle and spread the cold filling onto half of it lengthwise. Brush the edges of the pastry with cold water. Fold the pastry over to make a neat parcel (a large sausage roll shape) and seal well. Knock up the edges and seal the ends. Cut 3 vents in the roll with a pair of kitchen scissors and brush with beaten egg.

Cook at 220°C, 425°F, Gas Mark 7 for 20-25 minutes. Serve hot.

Fish Pie

Filling

12 oz haddock (thawed if frozen fish is used)	325 g haddock (thawed if frozen fish is used)
1 oz margarine	30 g margarine
1 onion peeled and chopped	1 onion peeled and chopped
4 oz mushrooms washed and sliced	100 g mushrooms washed and sliced
1 hardboiled egg finely chopped	1 hardboiled egg finely chopped
Salt and pepper	Salt and pepper
1/8 oz margarine	3 g margarine
1/8 oz plain flour	3 g plain flour
1/4 pt milk	150 ml milk

Shortcrust Pastry

4 oz plain flour	100 g plain flour
Pinch of salt	Pinch of salt
1 oz margarine	25 g margarine
1 oz lard	25 g lard
Cold water to mix	Cold water to mix

Filling

Dot the fish with ½ oz (15 g) of the margarine and steam it on a covered plate over a pan of boiling water for 20 minutes. When it is cooked flake the fish into a bowl removing any skin and bones.

Melt the remaining ½ oz (15 g) margarine in a small pan and gently fry the onion until it is soft and translucent but not brown. Stir in the mushrooms and cook until they turn colour. Drain and add to the fish. Stir in the chopped, hardboiled egg and season lightly. Put the fish mixture into a lightly greased pie dish.

Melt 1/8 oz (3 g) margarine in a pan, stir in 1/8 oz (3 g) plain flour, cook gently over a low heat for 2-3 minutes. Remove the pan from the heat and gradually stir in the milk taking care to keep the sauce smooth. Return the pan to the heat and bring to the boil stirring continuously. Lightly season the sauce and pour it over the fish.

Shortcrust Pastry

Sieve the flour and salt into a bowl. Rub in the margarine and lard and add enough cold water to mix to a firm dough. Knead gently for a few minutes to make a smooth pastry. Roll out thinly. Grease the edges of the pie dish and make a false rim on them with some pastry scraps. Put an upturned pottery egg cup in the centre of the pie dish to help to support the pastry. Cut the pastry to fit fit the dish. Dampen the edges and nip them together with the pastry forming the false rim. Knock the edges up. Cut 3 vents in the top of the pie with a pair of kitchen scissors.

Cook at 200°C, 400°F, Gas Mark 6 for 30-40 minutes.

Beef and Bean Pie

Filling

1 tin corned beef (12 oz)	1 tin corned beef (340 g)
1 tin kidney beans (15¼ oz) rinsed and drained	1 tin kidney beans (432 g) rinsed and drained
Salt and pepper	Salt and pepper
1 onion finely chopped	1 onion finely chopped

Shortcrust Pastry

8 oz plain flour	200 g plain flour
Pinch of salt	Pinch of salt
2 oz margarine	50 g margarine
2 oz lard	50 g lard
Cold water to mix	Cold water to mix

Filling

Flake the meat into a large bowl. Add the kidney beans, season lightly and stir in the onion.

Shortcrust Pastry

Sieve the flour and salt into a bowl, rub in the margarine and the lard and add enough cold water to mix to a firm dough. Knead gently for a few minutes to make a smooth pastry. Roll out half of the dough and line a lightly greased 9″ (23 cm) pie plate with it. Spoon the pie filling onto the pie plate. Roll out the remaining pastry and lay it on top of the plate, trim it to fit, dampen the edges and press them together to seal them. Cut 3 vents in the pie with a pair of kitchen scissors.

Cook for 30 minutes at 200°C, 400°F, Gas Mark 6.

Pork Cobbler

Casserole

1 oz margarine	25 g margarine
1 lb pork fillet trimmed and cut into 1″ cubes	450 g pork fillet trimmed and cut into 2.5 cm cubes
1 onion peeled and chopped	1 onion peeled and chopped
1 oz plain flour	25 g plain flour
¾ pt chicken stock	450 ml chicken stock
4 oz back bacon cut into 1″ squares	100 g back bacon cut into 2.5 cm squares
8 oz diced carrot	200 g diced carrot
½-1 tsp dried sage	½-1 tsp dried sage
Salt and pepper	Salt and pepper

Cobbler

2 oz S.R. flour	50 g S.R. flour
2 oz wholemeal flour	50 g wholemeal flour
Pinch of salt	Pinch of salt
1 oz margarine	25 g margarine
Milk to mix	Milk to mix

Casserole

Melt the margarine in a large pan and quickly fry the meat to brown it. When it is brown, drain it well and place it in a casserole dish. Gently fry the onion until it is soft and translucent but not brown. Stir in the flour and cook gently for 2-3 minutes. Remove the pan from the heat and gradually stir in the stock, taking care to keep the sauce smooth. Return the pan to the heat and bring to the boil stirring continuously. Add the bacon, carrot and dried sage and pour over the meat in the casserole dish. Season lightly.

Cover and cook at 180°C, 350°F, Gas Mark 4 for 45 minutes.

Cobbler

Mix the flours and salt together in a bowl. Rub in the margarine and mix to a stiff dough with a little milk. Knead for a few minutes to give a smooth texture. Roll out thinly on a floured surface and cut into circles with a scone cutter. Lay these on top of the meat after it has been in the oven for 45 minutes.

Cook uncovered for 15 minutes at 220°C, 425°F, Gas Mark 7.

Sweet Pies

Peaches and Cream Flan

Almond Pastry

2½ oz plain flour	65 g plain flour
2 oz margarine	50 g margarine
1½ oz ground almonds	40 g ground almonds
1 oz castor sugar	25 g castor sugar
1 egg yolk	1 egg yolk
¼ tsp almond essence	¼ tsp almond essence

Filling

1 tin peach halves (14½ oz)	1 tin peach halves (411 g)
¼ pt double cream	150 ml double cream
2 oz sieved icing sugar	50 g sieved icing sugar
A few drops of almond essence	A few drops of almond essence

Almond Pastry

Sieve the flour into a bowl and rub in the margarine. Stir in the ground almonds and the castor sugar. Add the egg yolk and almond essence and mix to a firm dough. Knead gently to make the pastry smooth. Roll out the pastry and line a 8″ (20.5 cm) flan dish with it. Bake blind at 190°C, 375°F, Gas Mark 5 for 10 minutes. Remove the greaseproof paper and the baking beans and bake for a further 5 minutes. Take the flan out of the oven and leave it to cool.

Filling

Drain the tin of peaches and arrange the fruit in the base of the flan. Mix the cream, icing sugar and almond essence together (but do not whisk) and pour over the peaches. Bake at 190°C, 375°F, Gas Mark 5 for 35-40 minutes. Cool in the tin on a wire rack.

Serve cold.

Birthday Pie

Almond Pastry

5 oz plain flour	125g plain flour
4 oz margarine	100 g margarine
3 oz ground almonds	75 g ground almonds
2 oz castor sugar	50 g castor sugar
2 egg yolks	2 egg yolks

Nut Layer

1½ oz flaked almonds	40 g flaked almonds

Fruit Layer

1 tin black cherries (15 oz) drained and stoned	1 tin black cherries (426 g) drained and stoned

Macaroon Layer

6 oz castor sugar	150 g castor sugar
6 oz ground almonds	150 g ground almonds
3 eggs	3 eggs
A little castor sugar for dredging	A little castor sugar for dredging

Almond Pastry

Sieve the flour into a bowl and rub in the margarine. Stir in the ground almonds and the castor sugar. Add the egg yolks and mix to a firm dough. Knead gently to make the pastry smooth. Roll out and line a lightly greased shallow 9″ (23 cm) round cake tin with it.

Nut Layer

Scatter the flaked almonds over the base of the pastry case.

Fruit Layer

Scatter the stoned cherries over the almonds.

Macaroon Layer

Mix the sugar and ground almonds together in a bowl. Beat in the whisked eggs. Spread this mixture over the cherries. Dredge lightly with castor sugar.

Bake at 190°C, 375°F, Gas Mark 5 for 35-40 minutes.

Chocolate and Walnut Flan

Chocolate Pastry

3½ oz plain flour	90 g plain flour
½ oz cocoa	15 g cocoa
Pinch of salt	Pinch of salt
3 oz margarine	75 g margarine
½ oz castor sugar	15 g castor sugar
1 egg yolk	1 egg yolk
A little water to mix	A little water to mix

Filling

2 oz margarine	50 g margarine
2 oz castor sugar	50 g castor sugar
1 egg	1 egg
1 oz S.R. flour	25 g S.R. flour
2 oz ground walnuts	50 g ground walnuts
(ground in a blender)	(ground in a blender)

Icing

4 oz icing sugar	100 g icing sugar
½ oz cocoa	15 g cocoa
1-2 tbsp warn water	1-2 tbsp warm water
Few drops vanilla essence	Few drops vanilla essence

Chocolate Pastry

Sieve the flour, cocoa and salt into a bowl, rub in the margarine and stir in the sugar. Add the egg yolk and enough cold water to mix to a firm dough. Knead lightly to give a smooth pastry, roll out and line a 7″ (18 cm) flan dish with it.

Filling

Cream the margarine and sugar together until they are soft and fluffy. Whisk the egg and beat it into the creamed mixture a little at a time. Carefully fold in the flour and the ground walnuts. Spoon the mixture into the flan dish and level it off.

Bake at 190°C, 375°F, Gas Mark 5 for 25-30 minutes or until it is nicely brown and firm to the touch. Leave to cool on a wire rack.

Icing

Sieve the icing sugar and cocoa into a bowl and mix with the water and the vanilla essence to a glacé icing consistency. Spread over the flan and leave to set.

Lemon and Almond Tarts

Almond Pastry

5 oz plain flour	125 g plain flour
4 oz margarine	100 g margarine
3 oz ground almonds	75 g ground almonds
2 oz castor sugar	50 g castor sugar
2 egg yolks	2 egg yolks
½ tsp almond essence	½ tsp almond essence

Filling

6-8 oz lemon curd	150-200 g lemon curd

Almond Pastry

Sieve the flour into a bowl and rub in the margarine. Stir in the ground almonds and the castor sugar. Add the egg yolks and the almond essence and mix to a firm dough. Knead gently to make the pastry smooth and roll out on a lightly floured surface. Cut out 34 pastry circles with a scone cutter. Lightly grease 17 patty tins and line them with 17 pastry circles.

Filling

Put teaspoonfuls of lemon curd into the patty tins. Put the pastry lids on and seal well.

Bake at 190°C, 375°F, Gas Mark 5 for 20 minutes. Cool in the tin for 30 minutes before turning them out onto a wire rack.

Royal Tarts

Shortcrust Pastry

6 oz plain flour	150 g plain flour
Pinch of salt	Pinch of salt
1½ oz margarine	40 g margarine
1½ oz lard	35 g lard
A little cold water to mix	A little cold water to mix

Filling

4 oz margarine	100 g margarine
4 oz castor sugar	100 g castor sugar
2 eggs	2 eggs
4 oz S.R. flour	100 g S.R. flour
A little milk to mix	A little milk to mix
2 oz finely chopped glacé cherries	50 g finely chopped glacé cherries
2 tbsp clear honey	2 tbsp clear honey

Icing

8 oz sieved icing sugar	225 g sieved icing sugar
A little warm water to mix	A little warm water to mix
4 finely chopped glacé cherries	4 finely chopped glacé cherries

Shortcrust Pastry

Sieve the flour and salt into a bowl. Rub in the margarine and lard and add enough cold water to make a firm dough. Knead gently to make a smooth pastry. Roll cut thinly, cut into circles with a scone cutter and line 24 patty tins with the pastry.

Filling

Cream the margarine and sugar until they are soft and fluffy. Lightly whisk the eggs and add them to the creamed mixture. Sieve the flour and fold it in. The mixture should be of a soft dropping consistency, if it is too stiff add a little milk. Put a little chopped cherry and clear honey into the base of each patty tin. Put teaspoonfuls of the cake mixture into the tarts. Bake at 190°C, 375°F, Gas Mark 5 for 25-30 minutes.

Icing

Mix the icing sugar with a little warm water and ice each tart. Decorate with a piece of glacé cherry.

Pineapple Pie

4 oz margarine	100 g margarine
8 oz crushed digestive biscuits	225 g crushed digestive biscuits
1 can condensed milk (14½ oz)	1 can condensed milk (410 g)
¼ pt double cream	150 ml double cream
1 oz castor sugar	15 g castor sugar
1 tin crushed pineapple (8 oz) drained	1 tin crushed pineapple (237 g) drained
½ oz gelatine	15 g gelatine
3 tbsp cold water	3 tbsp cold water
A little whipped cream to serve (optional)	A little whipped cream to serve (optional)

Melt the margarine in a pan and stir in the crushed biscuits. Press into a 9″ (23 cm) round cake tin. Put the condensed milk into a bowl. Whip the cream and the castor sugar in another bowl until the mixture peaks. Whisk the cream into the condensed milk. Stir in the crushed pineapple. Dissolve the gelatine in 3 tbsp of warm water in a bowl over a pan of hot water. Stir the gelatine into the mixture. Pile onto the biscuit base. Chill in the refrigerator until it is set. Serve on its own or with a little whipped cream.

We have probably already had the first frosts of the winter now and need extra energy for facing the cold days ahead. What better way of providing this than with some delicious winter puddings and desserts?

Apple Sauce and Dumplings

Apple Sauce

1 lb prepared cooking apples peeled, cored and sliced	450 g prepared cooking apples peeled, cored and sliced
2 oz granulated sugar	50 g granulated sugar
4 tbsp water	4 tbsp water

Dumplings

4 oz S.R. flour	100 g S.R. flour
Pinch of salt	Pinch of salt
2 oz shredded suet	50 g shredded suet
2 oz granulated sugar	50 g granulated sugar
Pinch of cinnamon	Pinch of cinnamon
Cold water for mixing	Cold water for mixing

Apple Sauce

Lightly grease a casserole dish. Put the apples into a pan and add the sugar and water. Cover and cook gently until the apples are pulpy. Pour them into the casserole dish.

Dumplings

Mix the flour, salt, suet, sugar and cinnamon together in a bowl. Add enough cold water to make a firm dough. Form the pastry into 6-8 balls and drop these into the apple purée. Cover and bake at 180°C, 350°F, Gas Mark 4 for 30-40 minutes.

Serve hot with custard.

Brazilian Crumble

1 tin apricot halves (15 oz)	1 tin apricot halves (425 g)
2 oz S.R. flour	50 g S.R. flour
2 oz wholemeal flour	50 g wholemeal flour
2 oz margarine	50 g margarine
1 oz dark muscovado sugar	25 g dark muscovado sugar
1 oz ground brazil nuts (ground in a blender)	25 g ground brazil nuts (ground in a blender)

Lightly grease a casserole dish. Drain the tin of apricots and arrange the fruit in the dish. Put the flours into a bowl. Rub in the margarine. Stir in the sugar and the ground brazil nuts. Scatter the crumble topping over the fruit.

Bake at 190°C, 375°F, Gas Mark 5 for 30-35 minutes until the crumble is lightly browned. Serve hot with custard.

Cherry and Almond Pudding with Honey Sauce

Cherry and Almond Pudding

4 oz margarine	100 g margarine
4 oz sugar	100 g sugar
2 eggs	2 eggs
4 oz S.R. flour	100 g S.R. flour
1 oz ground almonds	25 g ground almonds
1 oz chopped glacé cherries	25 g chopped glacé cherries
A little milk to mix	A little milk to mix

Honey Sauce

¾ oz cornflour	20 g cornflour
½ pt milk	300 ml milk
3 tbsp clear honey	3 tbsp clear honey

Cherry and Almond Pudding

Lightly grease a 1½ pt (900 ml) basin. Cream the margarine and the sugar together until they are soft and fluffy. Whisk the eggs and beat them into the creamed mixture a little at a time. Carefully fold in the flour, ground almonds and chopped cherries. The mixture should be of a soft, dropping consistency, if it is too stiff add a little milk. Spoon the mixture into the basin and make a small depression in the centre of it. Cover the basin with 2 layers of greased, greaseproof paper and a layer of foil and tie with string. Pleat the greaseproof paper to allow room for expansion. Steam the pudding for 1½ hours.

Honey Sauce

Blend the cornflour in a basin with a little of the milk until it is smooth. Heat the rest of the milk and pour it onto the cornflour. Return this to the pan and heat gently, stirring all of the time until it boils. Stir in the honey and serve with the pudding.

Walnut and Treacle Pudding

2 tbsp Tate & Lyle dark syrup	2 tbsp Tate & Lyle dark syrup
4 oz margarine	100 g margarine
4 oz soft brown sugar	100 g soft brown sugar
2 eggs	2 eggs
6 oz S.R. flour	150 g S.R. flour
1 oz chopped walnuts	25 g chopped walnuts
A little milk to mix	A little milk to mix

Grease a 1½ pt (900 ml) basin. Put the dark syrup in the base of this.

Cream the margarine and sugar together until they are soft and fluffy. Whisk the eggs and beat them into the creamed mixture a little at a time. Sieve the flour and carefully fold it in. Stir in the chopped walnuts. The mixture should be of a soft, dropping consistency, if it is too stiff add a little milk. Spoon the mixture into the basin and make a small depression in the centre of it. Cover the basin with 2 layers of greased greaseproof paper and a layer of foil and tie with string. Pleat the paper to allow room for expansion.

Steam for 1½ hours. Serve hot with custard.

Whipped Banana Pudding

2 tbsp custard powder	2 tbsp custard powder
1 pt milk	600 ml milk
1 oz sugar	25 g sugar
4 medium sized bananas	4 medium sized bananas
1 tbsp lemon juice	1 tbsp lemon juice
3 egg whites	3 egg whites
3 oz castor sugar	75 g castor sugar

Mix the custard powder in a bowl with a little of the milk and the sugar. Heat the rest of the milk, pour it into the bowl and stir well. Return to the pan and bring to the boil stirring continuously. Remove the pan from the heat.

Peel and slice the bananas into rings. Toss them in the lemon juice to prevent discolouration. Stir them into the custard and discard any remaining lemon juice. Pour the custard into a casserole dish and leave to cool.

Whisk the egg whites until they peak. Fold in the castor sugar a little at a time and whisk again until they are stiff. Swirl the meringue over the banana custard, taking care to take it right to the edges of the bowl.

Bake at 190°C, 375°F, Gas Mark 5 for 15-20 minutes or until the meringue is nicely browned.

Rhubarb Flapjack Pudding

1 tin rhubarb (1 lb 3 oz)	1 tin rhubarb (560 g)
2 oz margarine	50 g margarine
2 oz brown sugar	50 g brown sugar
1 tsp lemon juice	1 tsp lemon juice
1 tsp golden syrup	1 tsp golden syrup
2 oz rolled oats	50 g rolled oats
1 oz crushed cornflakes	25 g crushed cornflakes
1 oz coconut	25 g coconut

Drain the tin of rhubarb and arrange the fruit in a lightly greased casserole dish. Melt the margarine in a pan, add the sugar and stir carefully until it dissolves. Add the lemon juice and golden syrup. Stir in the rolled oats, cornflakes and coconut and stir well to make sure everything is evenly coated. Spread over the rhubarb.

Bake at 190°C, 375°F, Gas Mark 5 for 25 minutes. Serve hot with custard.

Lemon and Coconut Pudding

3 oz margarine	75 g margarine
3 oz sugar	75 g sugar
1 egg	1 egg
Grated rind of 1 lemon	Grated rind of 1 lemon
3 oz S.R. flour	75 g S.R. flour
1 oz coconut	25 g coconut
A little milk to mix	A little milk to mix

Cream the margarine and sugar together until they are soft and fluffy. Whisk the egg and beat it into the creamed mixture a little at a time. Beat in the lemon rind. Sieve the flour and carefully fold it in. Fold in the coconut. The mixture should be of a soft, dropping consistency, if it is too stiff add a little milk. Spoon into a lightly greased casserole dish.

Bake at 180°C, 350°F, Gas Mark 4 for 35-40 minutes. Serve hot with custard.

October 31st – Halloween

This was believed to be the night when ghosts and witches walked abroad and there are many customs linked to it. Some, like the lighting of bonfires, have died out. However, others are still flourishing. These include the Halloween games of bobbing and ducking for apples and the tradition of the turnip lantern for warding off evil spirits. Turnip lanterns are made by cutting the top off a turnip, scooping out the flesh, cutting holes for the eyes, nose and mouth, threading some string across the top for a handle, fixing a lighted candle in the turnip and putting the top on. These are then carried around the streets by children.

November

November 1st – All Saints Day (All Souls Eve)

On this night bonfires would be lit and children would go around the houses soul-caking. The soul cakes that they were given were either small fruit cakes or small spiced madeira cakes.

Soul Cakes

4 oz margarine	100 g margarine
4 oz castor sugar	100 g castor sugar
3 eggs	3 eggs
8 oz S.R. flour	200 g S.R. flour
Pinch of salt	Pinch of salt
1 tsp mixed spice	1 tsp mixed space
A little milk to mix	A little milk to mix

Cream the margarine and sugar together until they are soft and fluffy. Whisk the eggs and beat them into the creamed mixture a little at a time. Sieve the flour, salt and mixed spice together and carefully fold in. The mixture should be of a soft, dropping consistency, if it is too stiff add a little milk. Spoon the mixture into paper bun cases.

Bake at 180°C, 350°F, Gas Mark 4 for 30-40 minutes. Cool on a wire rack.

November 4th – Mischief Night

Tonight was the night for practical jokes, when youngsters would take gates from their hinges and hide them or remove door numbers and exchange them with different ones.

November 5th – Guy Fawkes' Night

This is the only fire festival that is still carried out all over England. As the bonfires burn with their guys on the top we remember Guy Fawkes and his unsuccessful attempt to blow up the King and Houses of Parliament in 1605. Guy Fawkes was born in York.

Gingerbread, or Parkin, is the traditional fayre of Guy Fawkes' Night so a suitable cake-cum-dessert to serve is Pineapple Gingerbread.

Pineapple Gingerbread

2 tbsp golden syrup	2 tbsp gold syrup
1 tin pineapple rings	1 tin pineapple rings
(15¼ oz)	(432 g)
5 oz wholemeal flour	125 g wholemeal flour
1 oz plain flour	25 g plain flour
1½ tsp ground ginger	1½ tsp ground ginger
1 tsp bicarbonate of soda	1 tsp bicarbonate of soda
3 oz soft brown sugar	75 g soft brown sugar
3 oz margarine	75 g margarine
3 tbsp black treacle	3 tbsp black treacle
1 tbsp golden syrup	1 tbsp golden syrup
2 eggs	2 eggs
⅛ pt milk	75 ml milk
Whipped cream to serve	Whipped cream to serve

Grease a 9″ (23 cm) deep, round cake tin. Put 2 tbsp golden syrup into the tin and spread it evenly over the base. Drain the tin of pineapple rings and arrange them on the golden syrup. Mix the flours, ginger, bicarbonate of soda and sugar in a bowl. Melt the margarine in a pan with the black treacle and 1 tbsp golden syrup. Pour this onto the dry ingredients and beat well. Lightly whisk the eggs and milk in a bowl and add them to the cake mixture. Beat well and pour on top of the pineapple rings. Bake at 180°C, 350°F, Gas Mark 4 for 45 minutes. Leave the cake in the tin for a few minutes before turning out onto a wire rack. Serve cold with whipped cream. This is a very attractive cake with its glazed pineapple rings on the top.

November 11th – Martinmas

St. Martin's Day is perhaps better known as Armistice Day when bright red poppies are worn.

Armistice Cake

4 oz S.R. flour	100 g S.R. flour
4 oz wholemeal flour	100 g wholemeal flour
Pinch of salt	Pinch of salt
1 tsp baking powder	1 tsp baking powder
4 oz margarine	100 g margarine
4 oz soft brown sugar	100 g soft brown sugar
2 oz sultanas	50 g sultanas
2 oz raisins	50 g raisins
2 oz chopped mixed peel	50 g chopped mixed peel
1 tsp mixed spice	1 tsp mixed spice
3 eggs	3 eggs

Put the flours, salt and baking powder into a bowl. Rub in the margarine, stir in the sugar, sultanas, raisins, mixed peel and mixed spice. Lightly whisk the eggs and beat them into the dry ingredients. Mix well. Lightly grease a 7″ (18 cm) deep, round cake tin and line it with greaseproof paper. Spoon the mixture into this. Bake at 180°C, 350°F, Gas Mark 4 for 1¼-1½ hours. Cook on a wire rack.

As the evenings become darker and colder it is a treat to relax by the fire and indulge in the luxury of a suppertime snack. These are perfect for a quick bite if you are either entertaining or just feeding the family. They are also so quick to make that they are sure to become the cook's favourites as well.

Pizza Snacks

½ oz margarine	15 g margarine
1 small onion peeled and chopped	1 small onion peeled and chopped
4 oz mushrooms washed and sliced	100 g mushrooms washed and slices
1 tin tomatoes (8 oz)	1 tin tomatoes (227 g)
Salt and pepper	Salt and pepper
4 oz ham cut into ½″ squares	100 g ham cut into 1.25 cm squares
12 crumpets	12 crumpets
3 oz grated cheese	75 g grated cheese

Melt the margarine in a pan and gently fry the onion until it is soft and translucent but not brown. Add the mushrooms and cook until they turn colour. Drain the tin of tomatoes, roughly chop, and stir them into the onion and mushroom mixture. Season lightly. Simmer gently uncovered for 15 minutes. Stir in the ham.

Toast the crumpets on their bases. Cover the tops with the topping and scatter on the cheese, grill until the cheese bubbles. If you like crumpets crispy then toast both sides before putting on the topping. Serve piping hot.

Leek and Bacon Baked Potatoes

4 large potatoes	4 large potatoes
1 oz margarine	25 g margarine
4 oz finely chopped leek	100 g finely chopped leek
4 oz back bacon chopped into 1″ squares	100 g back bacon chopped into 2.5 cm squares
1 oz margarine	25 g margarine
1 tbsp milk	1 tbsp milk
Salt and pepper	Salt and pepper

Scrub the potatoes clean and dry them. Prick them all over with a fork and bake them at 200°C, 400°F, Gas Mark 6 for 1¼-1¾ hours.

Before the potatoes are ready melt 1 oz (25 g) margarine in a pan and gently fry the leeks for 20 minutes in a covered pan. Add the bacon squares and cook for a further 5 minutes or until the bacon turns colour.

When the potatoes are cooked remove them from the oven, cut them in half lengthwise and gently spoon out the flesh taking care not to break the skins. Mash the potato with 1 oz (25 g) margarine and the milk and season lightly. When the potato is smooth mix in the bacon and leek. Press this into the skins and reheat under a medium grill.

Corned Beef Toasties

8 oz corned beef	225 g corned beef
1 small onion very finely chopped	1 small onion very finely chopped
2 tomatoes skinned and chopped	2 tomatoes skinned and chopped
Salt and pepper	Salt and pepper
8 slices of bread	8 slices of bread
A little butter for spreading	A little butter for spreading

Flake the corned beef into a bowl, stir in the onion and the tomatoes. Mix well and season lightly. Toast 4 slices of bread on one side, butter them on the uncooked side and spread with the mixture. Pop under the grill for a few minutes to warm through. Butter one side of the remaining slices and put them buttered side down onto the mixture. Toast until brown.

Stir-Up Sunday

This is the Sunday nearest St. Andrew's Day (November 30th) and traditionally it is the day when Christmas Puddings are made. The name may sound like an instruction to the busy cook but it is in fact taken from the Collect for the day, "Stir-up, we beseech Thee, O Lord, the wills of thy faithful people . . .". The rich Christmas Pudding that is enjoyed in so many homes on Christmas Day has quite a history and many customs attached to it. It began life as a savoury dish containing meat but became a sweet dessert in the early 1800s. It is considered lucky if everyone in the family stirs the pudding and makes a wish while it is being made. Various silver trinkets used to be added to the pudding before it was cooked and if the eater found a thimble it meant a single life, while a ring meant an imminent marriage. Traditionally the pudding was carried to the table bathed in brandy flames which perhaps were a symbol of the great bonfires which used to be lit at this dark time of the year.

Christmas Pudding

4 oz S.R. flour	100 g S.R. flour
2 oz wholemeal flour	50 g wholemeal flour
Pinch of salt	Pinch of salt
1 level tsp mixed spice	1 level tsp mixed spice
½ level tsp ground nutmeg	½ level tsp ground nutmeg
6 oz soft light brown sugar	150 g soft light brown sugar
2 oz glacé cherries chopped	50 g glacé cherries chopped
4 oz ground almonds	100 g ground almonds
4 oz shredded suet	100 g shredded suet
1 dessert apple peeled, cored and finely chopped	1 dessert apple peeled, cored and finely chopped
4 oz wholemeal breadcrumbs	100 g wholemeal breadcrumbs
6 oz raisins	150 g raisins
8 oz sultanas	200 g sultanas
6 oz currants	150 g currants
2 oz flaked almonds	50 g flaked almonds
3 oz mixed peel	75 g mixed peel
3 eggs	3 eggs
¼ pt milk	150 ml milk
2 tbsp brandy	2 tbsp brandy
Finely grated rind and juice of 1 orange	Finely grated rind and juice of 1 orange
2 tbsp lemon juice	2 tbsp lemon juice
2 tbsp black treacle	2 tbsp black treacle

Put the flours, salt, mixed spice and nutmeg into a bowl and mix thoroughly. Stir in the sugar, cherries, ground almonds, suet, apple, breadcrumbs, dried fruits, almonds and mixed peel. Lightly whisk the eggs and milk together and add to the dry ingredients. Beat well and stir in the brandy, orange juice, orange rind, lemon juice and black treacle. Grease two 1 pt (600 ml) basins. Pack the bowls with the pudding mixture. Cover with two layers of greased, greaseproof paper and a layer of foil and tie with string. Steam for 7 hours. Cool, remove the paper, remove the puddings from the bowls and wrap in dry greaseproof paper. Store in a dry place. Steam for a further 2 hours before eating.

If you have a pressure cooker: steam without weights for 15 minutes; cook at high pressure for 1¾ hours. Store as stated. Before eating cook at high pressure for 20 minutes.

December 24th – Christmas Eve

In times past this was the day when the huge Yule Log was dragged from the local wood into the home. It was lit in the evening and would burn throughout the Christmas period. The remnants of this great log were saved until the following year when they would be used as kindling to set fire to the next Yule Log. The ashes were also kept as it was believed that they were lucky and would protect the house from fire. Nowadays very few of us have a genuine Yule Log, but many of us quite happily tuck into a confectionary one!

In Dewsbury, an ancient custom dating back 700 years is carried out on this night when the church bell is rung once for every year since Christ's birth. This is known as Tolling the Devil's Knell. The bell that is rung is called Black Tom of Soothill, after the man who donated it in the thirteenth century as a penance for murdering a servant.

December 25th – Christmas Day

This is still a great day for feasting just as it has always been although our Christmas fayre has changed over the years. In medieval times the Boar's Head was a firm favourite. It was carried from the kitchen to the hall in a great procession and was certainly the highlight of the meal. Along with this were served all kinds of roasted birds. Turkeys were unknown in this country until 1542 when they were introduced from North America but by 1800 they were very popular.

Like the Christmas Pudding, mince pies were originally savoury although nowadays they are sweet. They were also oval in shape which probably symbolized Christ's manger in the stable. A rather fattening custom concerning this delicacy is the one that says that a mince pie should be eaten on each of the Twelve Days of Christmas to guarantee good fortune in the coming year. It is always a good excuse for extra eating, if nothing else! Marzipan and gingerbread are other traditional sweetmeats of this time.

December 26th – Boxing Day

This was the day when Christmas presents were given to servants. The rather peculiar name may have come from the Church alms-boxes, which were opened today and their contents distributed to the poor, or from the boxes that the apprentices took from door to door before Christmas and opened on this day.

At such a festive time the accent must be on more luxurious dishes which are suitable for any special occasion.

Starters

Mushrooms with Cream and Brandy

1 oz margarine	25 g margarine
1 small onion peeled and finely chopped	1 small onion peeled and finely chopped
8 oz mushrooms washed and sliced	225 g mushrooms washed and sliced
2 tbsp brandy	2 tbsp brandy
Salt and pepper	Salt and pepper
1 tbsp single cream	1 tbsp single cream
4 slices of wholemeal bread	4 slices of wholemeal bread

Melt the margarine in a pan and gently fry the onion until it is soft and translucent but not brown. Add the mushrooms and continue frying until they turn colour. Add the brandy and season lightly. Cover and simmer gently for 10 minutes. Remove the pan from the heat, stir in the cream and serve on slices of wholemeal toast.

Prawns and Almonds

½ oz margarine	15 g margarine
½ small onion peeled and very finely chopped	½ small onion peeled and very finely chopped
1 oz flaked almonds	25 g flaked almonds
4 oz peeled prawns (thawed and drained if frozen prawns are used)	100 g peeled prawns (thawed and drained if frozen prawns are used)
Salt and pepper	Salt and pepper

Melt the margarine in a pan and gently fry the onion until it is soft and translucent but not brown. Stir in the almonds and fry until they turn pale brown. Stir in the prawns. Reheat and season lightly. Serve hot with triangles of wholemeal bread.

Tuna Cocktail

1 tin tuna (7 oz)	1 tin tuna (198 g)
2 tbsp thousand island dressing	2 tbsp thousand island dressing
Salt and pepper	Salt and pepper
1 grapefruit peeled, cut into segments, membrane removed and roughly chopped	1 grapefruit peeled, cut into segments, membrane removed and roughly chopped
A little iceberg lettuce shredded	A little iceberg lettuce shredded

Drain the tin of tuna and flake the fish into a bowl. Stir in the thousand island dressing and season lightly. Add the prepared grapefruit and mix well. Line 4 small dishes with some of the shredded lettuce, put spoonfuls of the tuna mixture onto the lettuce. Serve with brown bread and butter.

Main Course

Beef Dijon

4 pieces of fillet steak each weighing approximately 6 oz	4 pieces of fillet steak each weighing approximately 150 g
2 oz butter	50 g butter
4 tsp Dijon mustard	4 tsp Dijon mustard

Beat the steaks betweens two pieces of non-stick baking parchment with a rolling pin to flatten them until they are double their original size. Heat the butter and mustard in a frying pan and fry the meat until it is brown on both sides. Brush four pieces of foil with the butter and put the meat on the foil. Wrap up into neat parcels. Lay these on a baking sheet.

Cook at 220°C, 425°F, Gas Mark 7 for 30 minutes.

Plaice with Orange Sauce

4 fillets of plaice	4 fillets of plaice
1 oz melted butter	25 g melted butter
½ oz margarine	15 g margarine
½ oz plain flour	15 g plain flour
¼ pt pure orange juice	150 ml pure orange juice
Salt and pepper	Salt and pepper

Brush the fish with the melted butter and season lightly. Arrange each fillet on a piece of buttered foil. Wrap into neat parcels and put onto a baking tray. Cook at 190°C, 375°F, Gas Mark 5 for 25 minutes. Melt ½ oz (15 g) margarine in a pan. Stir in the flour and cook for 2-3 minutes. Remove the pan from the heat and gradually stir in the orange juice taking care to keep the sauce smooth. Return the pan to the heat and bring to the boil, stirring continuously. Season lightly and serve with the fish.

Stuffed Pork Fillet

6 oz onions peeled and chopped	150 g onions peeled and chopped
1-1½ oz butter	25-35 g butter
3 level tsp dried sage	3 level tsp dried sage
3 oz white breadcrumbs	75 g white breadcumbs
Salt and pepper	Salt and pepper
1 lb pork fillet	450 g pork fillet
½ oz melted butter	15 g melted butter

Cook the onions in boiling, salted water for 15-20 minutes. Drain and put them into a bowl. Melt the butter in a small pan and pour it over the onions. Add the sage and breadcrumbs and mix well. Season lightly. Cut the pork fillet halfway through lengthwise and flatten it out a little by beating it with a rolling pin between sheets of non-stick baking parchment. Lay the meat on a board and brush both sides with the melted butter. Spread ⅔rds of the stuffing mixture down the centre. Roll the meat up around the stuffing and tie with fine string. Wrap the meat in some buttered foil and place it on a baking tray.

Cook at 180°C, 350°F, Gas Mark 4 for 1¼ hours. Serve the remaining stuffing with the meat.

Veal with Mushroom Sauce

2 oz butter	50 g butter
1 onion peeled and chopped	1 onion peeled and chopped
4 oz mushrooms washed and sliced	100 g mushrooms washed and sliced
1 oz plain flour	25 g plain flour
½ pt chicken stock	300 ml chicken stock
Salt and pepper	Salt and pepper
4 escalopes of veal	4 escalopes of veal
2 tbsp single cream	2 tbsp single cream

Melt 1 oz (25 g) of the butter in a pan and gently fry the onions until they are soft and translucent but not brown. Add the mushrooms and fry until they turn colour. Stir in the flour and cook for 2-3 minutes, remove the pan from the heat and gradually stir in the chicken stock, taking care to keep the sauce smooth. Season lightly. Return the pan to the heat and bring to the boil stirring continuously. Cover and simmer gently for 15 minutes.

Melt the remaining 1 oz (25 g) of butter in a separate pan and fry the veal for 5 minutes per side. Lift the meat out of the pan and keep it warm,

Stir the cream into the sauce, reheat and serve with the veal.

Trout with Gooseberry Sauce

4 rainbow trout
1 oz melted butter
Salt and pepper
Gooseberry Sauce
4 tbsp gooseberry jam
2 tbsp water
4 tbsp wine vinegar
Generous pinch of mixed
    herbs
Salt and pepper

4 rainbow trout
25 g melted butter
Salt and pepper

4 tbsp gooseberry jam
2 tbsp water
4 tbsp wine vinegar
Generous pinch of mixed
    herbs
Salt and pepper

Brush the trout with the melted butter and season lightly. Arrange each fish on a piece of buttered foil. Wrap into neat parcels. Put these parcels on a baking tray.

Cook at 190°C, 375°F, Gas Mark 5 for 25 minutes.

Gooseberry Sauce

Heat the gooseberry jam, water and wine vinegar in a pan and season with the mixed herbs and a little salt and pepper. Serve with the trout.

Desserts

Dessert Roulade

Roulade
4 oz plain dessert
    chocolate
2 tbsp strong black coffee
4 egg yolks

100 g plain dessert
    chocolate
2 tbsp strong black coffee
4 egg yolks

5 oz castor sugar
3 egg whites
Filling
¼ pt double cream
1 oz castor sugar
1 tbsp white rum
A little icing sugar for
    dusting

125 g castor sugar
3 egg whites

150 ml double cream
25 g castor sugar
1 tbsp white rum
A little icing sugar for
    dusting

Roulade

Grease and line a swiss roll tin with non-stick baking parchment. In a bowl over a pan of hot water melt the chocolate in the strong black coffee. Whisk the egg yolks and the castor sugar until they are thick and pale. Add the melted chocolate and coffee to the egg yolk mixture and beat well. Whisk the egg whites until they peak, then gently fold them into the mixture. Spoon the mixture into the lined tin and level the surface. Bake at 180°C, 350°F, Gas Mark 4 for 15 minutes. Leave in the tin and cool on a wire rack. After 10 minutes cover it with a clean, damp tea towel. Leave overnight.

Filling

Whip the cream, sugar and rum until it is stiff. Take the cake out of the tin and lay it on a piece of greaseproof paper which has been dusted with icing sugar. Cover the cake with the whipped cream. Roll up as you would a swiss roll, using the greaseproof paper to push the cake over. Dust with icing sugar and serve. This is a deliciously sticky cake but it is a little tricky and must be kept covered with a damp cloth to stop it going hard and unable to roll.

Victorian Babas

Babas

6 oz margarine	150 g margarine
6 oz castor sugar	150 g castor sugar
3 eggs	3 eggs
6 oz S.R. flour	150 g S.R. flour
A little milk to mix	A little milk to mix

Rum Syrup

¾ pt water	450 ml water
8 oz granulated sugar	225 g granulated sugar
4 tbsp rum	4 tbsp rum

Topping

½ pt whipping cream	300 ml whipping cream
2 oz castor sugar	50 g castor sugar
2 tins fruit cocktail (14½ oz) drained	2 tins fruit cocktail (410 g) drained

Babas

Cream the margarine and sugar together until they are soft and fluffy. Whisk the eggs and gradually beat them into the creamed mixture. Sieve the flour and carefully fold it in. The mixture should be of a soft, dropping consistency, if it is too stiff add a little milk. Spoon into a lightly greased and lined 9″ (23 cm) round cake tin and leave a slight hollow in the centre.

Bake at 180°C, 350°F, Cas Mark 4 for 45-50 minutes. Cool on a wire rack.

Rum Syrup

Heat the water and sugar together in a pan until the sugar dissolves. Remove the pan from the heat and add the rum. Put the cooled cake onto a plate and pour the syrup over it. Leave to soak overnight.

Topping

Whip the cream and sugar together until they peak.

Serve the cake in slices with the fruit cocktail spooned over them and a generous helping of cream.

Ginger Roll

1 pt strong black coffee	600 ml strong black coffee
1 pkt ginger nut biscuits (7.05 oz)	1 pkt ginger nut biscuits (200 g)
½ pt double cream	300 ml double cream
4 tbsp Tia Maria	4 tbsp Tia Maria
2 oz castor sugar	50 g castor sugar
2 egg whites	2 egg whites
2 oz plain dessert chocolate grated	50 g plain dessert chocolate grated

Put the black coffee into a pan and bring it to the boil. One by one carefully submerge the biscuits in the coffee. Leave them in the pan only for a fraction of a second and lift them out with a fish slice. Put them on a sheet of foil to cool. When all of the biscuits have been dipped whisk the cream, Tia Maria and the sugar until the mixture is just beginning to stiffen. Whisk the egg whites until they peak then carefully fold them into the cream mixture. Carefully sandwich the biscuits together with half of the cream mixture and arrange them on a plate in the shape of a roll. Spread the remaining cream over the biscuit roll and sprinkle with the grated chocolate.

Serve immediately.

INDEX

Starters — **Page Number**
Chicken Liver Pâté — 6
Courgette Starter — 17
Kipper Pâte — 6
Mushrooms with Cream and Brandy — 67
Prawns and Almonds — 67
Stuffed Harboiled Eggs — 28
Tuna Cocktail — 67

Soups
Chestnut Soup — 8
Courgette Soup — 9
Economy Tomato Soup — 9
Frankfurter Soup — 8
Kitchen Garden Soup — 10
Smoked Haddock and Bacon Soup — 10

Main Courses
Beef
Beef Dijon — 67
Beefy Pancakes — 14
Black and Beefy Stew — 23
Mince Casserole — 25
Veal with Mushroom Sauce — 68

Chicken
Chicken and Almond Casserole — 25

Eggs
Curried Omelette — 29
Potato Nests — 29
Savoury Flan — 30

Fish
Plaice with Orange Sauce — 68
Trout with Gooseberry Sauce — 69

Lamb
Brandied Liver and Bacon — 24

Pork
Cheese and Bacon Pancakes — 14
Italian Squares — 47
Pork Fillet with Parsnip and Apple — 24

Sausage Pizza — 46
Sausage Risotto — 24
Stuffed Pork Fillet — 68

Vegetarian
Country Fry-Up — 17
Pancake Lasagne — 16
Southern Supper — 18
Vegetable Medley — 18

Salads
Main Course Salads
Beefy Salad — 31
Dijon Salad — 33
Friday's Salad — 32
Quick Salmon Salad — 32
Supper Salad — 34
Tuna Salad — 33

Accompanying Salads
Bean and Rice Salad — 34
Club Salad — 35
Colourful Potato Salad — 36
Fruity Side Salad — 35
Mushroom and Walnut Salad — 35
Pineapple Salad with Curry Dressing — 36

Savoury Pies and Tarts
Beef and Bean Pie — 54
Cheesy Meat Pie — 52
Chicken Vol-au-Vents — 53
Chicken Wellingtons — 52
Fish Pie — 54
Individual Shepherd's Pies — 51
Mince Savoury Roll — 53
Pork Cobbler — 55
Sausage and Egg Pie — 38
Savoury Flan — 30
Tuna and Cheese Pasties — 38
Tuna Savouries — 5

Snacks and Supper Dishes
Bacon and Tomato Scramble — 29
Baked Ham and Eggs — 28

Beef Collops — 13
Corned Beef Toasties — 64
Cucumber and Cottage Cheese Buns — 37
Delicatessen Ham Sandwiches — 38
Leek and Bacon Baked Potatoes — 64
Pizza Snacks — 64
Ploughman's Extras — 37
Prawn Sandwiches — 37

Desserts
Apple Sauce and Dumplings — 59
Black Cherry and Chocolate Trifle — 41
Brazilian Crumble — 59
Cherry and Almond Pancakes — 15
Cherry and Almond Pudding with Honey Sauce — 60
Chocolate Banana Special — 42
Christmas Pudding — 65
Date and Ginger Pudding — 27
Dessert Roulade — 69
Ginger Roll — 70
Gooseberry and Ginger Crunch — 43
Ice Cream and Butterscotch Sauce — 42
Lemon and Coconut Pudding — 61
Midsummer Fancy — 45
Mocha Mousse — 43
Normandy Syllabub — 43
Orchard Soufflé — 30
Pineapple with Brandy and Orange Sauce — 40
Raspberry Dream — 45
Rhubarb Flapjack Pudding — 61
Scrumpy Strawberry Trifle — 44
Strawberry Snow — 44
Strawberry Sunrise — 44
Tipsy Fruit Salad — 45
Victorian Babas — 70
Walnut and Treacle Pudding — 60
Whipped Banana Pudding — 60

Biscuits, Cakes and Gateaux
Almond Ring — 48
Armistice Cake — 63
Banana Tea Loaf — 50
Chocolate Fudge Cake — 20

Date and Hazelnut Cake	26	Tea-Time Special	22	**Confectionary**
Date and Honey Scones	26	Uncle Sam's Brownies	40	Almond Kisses 11
Ginger Creams	20	Walnut and Cherry Upsidedown Cake	22	Butterscotch Creams 12
Honey Cake	39	Wholemeal Rock Buns	22	Coconut Favourites 12
Lemon Biscuits	40			Coffee Cream Bonbons 12
No-Bake Crispies	19	**Sweet Pies and Tarts**		
Pancake Gateaux	16	Apple and Mincemeat Pie	6	**Cocktail Savouries**
Peanut Butter Cake	19	Birthday Pie	56	Cheese Dominoes 5
Pineapple Gingerbread	63	Chocolate and Walnut Flan	57	Tuna Savouries 5
Simnel Cake	21	Lemon and Almond Tarts	57	
Soul Cakes	62	Mincemeat Meringue Tarts	7	**Miscellaneous**
Sweet Chelsea Buns	48	Peaches and Cream Flan	56	Breakfast Bonanza 27
Swiss Bars	39	Pineapple Pie	58	Cheese and Marmite Bread 47
Tea-Time Loaf	49	Royal Tarts	58	